FACTORING 101:
A Broker's Guide

Learn How to Earn Life-of-Account Residual Commission Income as an Industry Freelance Factoring Broker

Robert McMahon

ISBN 978-0-692-56610-7

Printed in the United States of America
First Printing November 2015

Trademarks

Various names used by companies to distinguish their software or other products are used throughout this text. These names can be claimed as trademarks. Such names and are used for editorial purposes only by the publisher with no intention of trademark violation. All such references to trademarked software or products are in initial capital letters or ALL CAPITAL letters. Individual companies should be contacted for complete information regarding trademarks and registration.

Disclaimer

This publication is designed to provide accurate and authoritative information in regards to the subject matter covered. It is sold with the understanding that the publisher is not engaged in the rendering of legal, accounting, tax, or other professional services or advice. If legal, accounting, tax or any professional services are required, competent professional council should be sought.

Published by
DataMax Marketing Systems, Inc.

11000 Metro Pkwy
Suite 22
Ft. Myers, FL 33966

TRADEMARKED TERMS REFERENCED IN THIS GUIDE

QuickBooks® is a registered trademark of Intuit, Inc.
Excel® is a registered trademark of the Microsoft Corporation
Word® is a registered trademark of the Microsoft Corporation
Publisher® is a registered trademark of the Microsoft Corporation
PowerPoint® is a registered trademark of the Microsoft Corporation
Google® is a registered trademark of Google Inc.
Google Analytics® is a registered trademark of Google Inc.
InDesign® is a registered trademark of Adobe Systems Incorporated
PaperDirect® is a registered trademark of Paper Direct, Inc.
StockLayouts® is a registered trademark of StockLayouts LLC
LinkedIn® is a registered trademark of LinkedIn Corporation
Facebook® is a registered trademark of Facebook Inc.
Toastmasters® is a registered trademark of Toastmasters International
Rotary® is a registered trademark of Rotary International
Kiwanis® is a registered trademark of Kiwanis International
Elks® is a registered trademark of the Benevolent and Protective Order of the Elks
Lions® is a registered trademark of the International Association of Lions Clubs
Craigslist® is a registered trademark of Craigslist, Inc.
Packers® is a registered trademark of The Green Bay Packers

Table of Contents

Preface

Welcome to Factoring! The business opportunity you are about to explore, that of *factoring broker,* is exceptional by any measure. Whether your ultimate goal in purchasing this study guide is to enter the industry as a full time career professional or you are simply seeking to expand your industry knowledge to supplement the income from a current profession, you will find this industry offers a unique opportunity to earn an exceptional income while also enjoying a high degree of prestige and vocational respectability. For all who successfully enter, it is a career which can be both personally and financially rewarding.

If you haven't noticed, the economic climate in America has changed dramatically in the past three decades. The once vibrant manufacturing sector in America is no more than a shadow of its past glory, with China's economy and GDP now poised to surpass that of our own. And while headline unemployment figures may suggest a modestly recovering domestic economy, there is a great deal more to that story. As of this writing, there are roughly 95 million individuals who have left the American labor force. Now standing at just over 62.4%, the U.S. Bureau of Labor Statistics confirms this is the lowest labor force participation rate since 1978. With the scarcity of jobs offering a true living wage being well documented, more and more Americans are now realizing the path to personal recovery is to launch some type of entrepreneurial business of their own.

Those making the decision to enter the world of the entrepreneur and start their own enterprise are faced with many hurdles and challenges in today's economy. Most new business operators struggle to accumulate the seed capital to buy equipment, inventory, and finally open their doors, only to then find themselves faced with an even greater challenge, the need for ready working capital once the business becomes operational. Historically, such capital has been provided through community banks. But as everyone in business today is well aware, banks simply aren't lending. And, that is a statistic which is very unlikely to change in the foreseeable future.

Successfully entering the factoring industry as a freelance consultant or "factoring broker" means you will be performing a valuable financial service to small and mid-size business owners by assisting in the sourcing of ready financial alternatives to traditional bank loans and lines of credit. Factoring industry brokers are true financial consultants in every sense of the word. They earn fee and commission income based on their in-depth knowledge and understanding of the various forms of factoring and alternative types of commercial finance which can be brought to bear to solve a particular small business capital problem. And just as important, they have developed the marketing skills to convey that knowledge to small business entrepreneurs in need.

Very few individuals entering this industry come initially equipped with the required product knowledge and marketing skills to immediately succeed. Factoring is a very specialized form of asset-based finance and regardless of education or past professional experience, most entering the industry will begin at the same neophyte level of expertise. Fortunately, in spite of its worldwide recognition as one of the most powerful forms of commercial finance available to small business owners, factoring is also characterized by its transactional simplicity. For most, the learning curve to acquire the necessary product knowledge to compete as an industry broker will be very short.

Entering the factoring industry as a freelance broker represents an exceptional business opportunity and career path for those individuals who can describe themselves as entrepreneurial "self-starters" or mobile creatives. Though a well practiced vocation in Europe, this unique area of consulting continues to remain well under-the-radar in the U.S. It is a very specialized area of small business finance and for the most part, you will find competition to be very light in most communities, if it exists at all. Do not, however, look at this opportunity as the latest highly promoted get rich quick scheme. Many do, only to find that this area of consulting, like almost all others, will take much hard work, patience, and determination for success.

It is very true that the fee and commission compensation paid to industry freelance brokers by factors and related lenders for referrals is extraordinary by any measure. To participate and earn such fees and commissions, you will need to acquire a reasonably high level of product knowledge and probably also develop certain marketing skills. As you may already be aware, however, locating sources of truly affordable training for this career path has been historically difficult and often quite expensive. But, that has changed. *Factoring 101: A Broker's Guide* is designed to provide you with all the basic industry knowledge you will require to enter this unique vocation and exceptional area of specialized consulting both successfully and profitably at a truly minimal cost.

About This Guide

Factoring 101: A Broker's Guide is provided through the *International Association of Commercial Finance Brokers* (IACFB) and its purpose is to assist those interested in entering the industry with learning the business and entering successfully. Building a comprehensive working knowledge of factoring, the asset-based finance industry, and its many niches and facets is essential to success. Absorbing this guide's contents will expand your capabilities and help you to enter this unique industry well prepared.

This training guide presents the industry from an independent broker's prospective. Because you will be earning your income from client referrals, it naturally focuses heavily on business development rather than factoring's rather complex operational side. To accomplish your sales tasks as a freelance industry broker, however, you will need to know a few operational characteristics of factoring as well and these are provide for you as required. Additionally, a good industry broker can often be a factor's first line of defense against fraud. Knowing a bit about the normal day-to-day operational side of factoring will dramatically increase your ability to detect fraudulent client applications, activities, and expand your value as a broker to your factors.

The Factoring 101 Program at IACFB

This guide is the basic training component IACFB's Factoring 101 Program for new industry consultants. The second part of Factoring 101, the "**Business-in-a-Box**" marketing support component, is offered by Campus IACFB's Annex through subscription. It includes essentially everything you will need to open and launch your business from the marketing side. The Campus Annex **Business-in-a-Box** subscription will provide you with:

- a professionally designed consultant website
- a business email
- brochure and flyer templates (PDF format)
- access to IACFB's Directory of Lenders (over 500 broker-friendly industry lenders)
- pre-formatted *PowerPoint* workshop presentations and handouts
- downloadable case studies (PDF format) and lead-generating offers

The Campus Annex subscription is optional and provides a great deal of support for those without the required skills (or time) to design, write, format, and research the marketing and support materials necessary to start and launch their consultancy. Additional information on the Campus Annex and current subscription information can be found in the back of this text and also at the IACFB's public website at www.iacfb.org.

The Factoring Broker Forums

Additional support for new industry brokers can be found at the *IACFB's Factoring 101 Forums.* These forums were specifically created to support the *Factoring 101 Training Program* and will provide you with an easily accessible online venue where you can ask questions about the guide's contents, the factoring business, and the ABF industry. The *Factoring 101 Forums* also house the *Learning Lab* with many broker support items for you including a "Lenders Presentations" archive filled with showcased MP3 recordings made by factors and many other lenders to IACFB members over the past several years. As a purchaser of this guide, you will have free *Learning Lab* access and receive notices and invitations to attend future IACFB sponsored lender presentations made month to month. Registration to the forums is free and you can sign up and join the community by visiting the forums at www.factoringbrokerforums.com

The Factoring 101 Glossary of Terms

Throughout the guide you may come across words you are unfamiliar with as certain subjects and topics are initially introduced. Occasionally, such words represent important industry terminology or concepts which you should know and understand as a broker. They are included in the guide's support glossary located at the *Learning Lab.*

The Factoring 101 Proficiency / Certification Exam

One of the greatest fears common to all new brokers is that they do not know enough to comfortably network with loan officers, accountants and other local professionals effectively. In short, they fear they will be exposed as a novice. Naturally, one of your goals as an industry broker is to be looked upon as a small business finance expert in your local community so you can benefit from professional referrals.

The *Factoring 101 Proficiency Exam* is designed to give you the confidence you will need when networking and building relationships with local sources of business referral. Put simply, if you can score 85% or higher on the proficiency exam, you are ready to launch your business and comfortably network with anyone. The exam is free and provided through *Class Marker.* When you feel you are ready to test your skills after studying and absorbing the materials in this text, there is a direct link to the exam in the *Learning Lab.*

FACTORING 101: INTRODUCTION

Welcome to Factoring

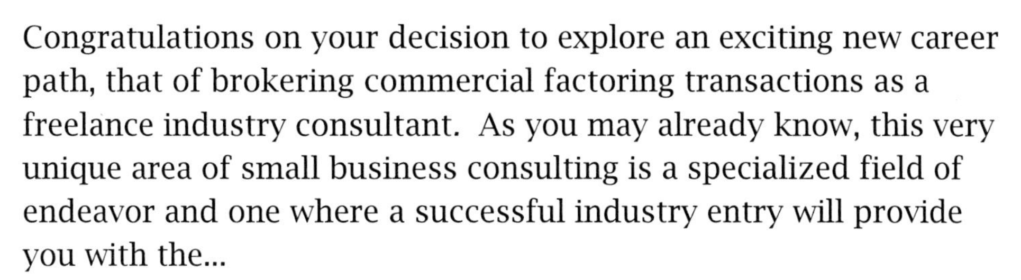
Congratulations on your decision to explore an exciting new career path, that of brokering commercial factoring transactions as a freelance industry consultant. As you may already know, this very unique area of small business consulting is a specialized field of endeavor and one where a successful industry entry will provide you with the...

- **flexibility to reside and earn a living from virtually anywhere or anyplace.**
- **personal freedom to custom tailor your hours and to work as much or as little as you desire.**
- **ability to enjoy a highly regarded professional status within your community and by all you meet.**

HIGHLY REGARDED PROFESSIONAL STATUS

What is most important, a career as an industry consultant will provide you with the opportunity to earn the near-legendary fee and commission income that has made the industry famous.

Your earnings as a broker will only be defined by the:

- **product knowledge you acquire**
- **hours you devote weekly to developing business**
- **networking opportunities you engage in**
- **direct marketing skills you develop**

Industry Opportunities

OPPORTUNITY OF A LIFETIME

Before you throw yourself head first into what you may have heard is the "opportunity of a lifetime", you should probably develop a little better understanding of just what this business is all about and how you, as an independent freelance consultant, fit into it.

First of all, this is a large industry brimming with opportunity and excitement. It is a tailor-made career path for certain types of individuals we will refer to as "entrepreneurial self-starters". In fact, worldwide, *asset-based finance* is such an enormous industry you may come to wonder just how you knew so little about it and the many lucrative income-generating opportunities it offers to almost anyone willing to do a little research and exploration. And, though you may currently know very little about the industry's various inner workings and intricacies, we can assure you tht learning more about it is very much worth the time and effort you will put forth to gain a little industry working knowledge.

For you, the reader and soon to be factoring broker, this career path is all about being an industry "middleman" whose business involves periodically referring cash-strapped small business owners in need of financing to an appropriate industry lender. In doing so, you will earn a referral commission or fee paid by that lender. Does it sound simple? Well, believe it or not, it actually is. But an important part of that conversation is that very few people are aware of just how lucrative that fee and commission income can be. And, though you may have heard the business simply referred to as one of "brokering", there is really quite a bit more to that story.

From a truly professional and career oriented viewpoint, you are entering a high profile freelance consulting business that will require you to develop a significant level of industry product knowledge as well as cultivate certain soft skills needed for developing business. Consulting, as a profession, is one of the most rapidly expanding areas of opportunity in today's job marketplace. This particular area of consulting, with its focus on small business finance alternatives, represents one of the highest levels of "specialty" consultant opportunity.

So What Are You?

ALTERNATIVE TO BANK FINANCING

Accounts receivable factoring is just one of many specialized forms or types of alternative commercial finance (alternative to traditional bank financing) found throughout the world and as mentioned, it is provided by members of the asset-based finance community of lenders. This highly regarded group of financiers is comprised of many unique, and sometimes unconventional, capital providers and may even include several institutions right in your local community.

AN INDEPENDENT FACTORING BROKER

Well, get ready! After absorbing the contents of this guide and completing its exams, you will be poises to join this prestigious community as a member of its most important part, the business development area. You will become a commissioned agent or what is more commonly termed by those in the industry, a *freelance factoring broker,* a profession of exceptional opportunity, practiced by only a few, and well under-the-radar when it comes to measuring serious competition.

Serving Two Clients

As an independent factoring broker, you are a commissioned lead generator. You are a transactional middleman and will actually serve two specific clients. These are the:

- **Business Owner**...where you will act as an knowledgeable business finance consultant.
- **Factor**...where you will act as a freelance independent contractor for business development.

FREELANCE INDEPENDENT CONTRACTOR

Types of Consultants

Consultants, from the Latin *consultare* meaning "to discuss", are professionals who provide expert advice based on their above average experience or knowledge regarding a specialized field, process, or product. Operationally, consultants can either be:

- **Internal:** someone on permanent staff and available for consultation with others in a daily business, or...
- **External:** an independent contractor whose expertise is usually employed only on a temporary basis and as it is periodically required.

There are many types of consultants found in the world today and certainly one of the driving forces behind the dramatic growth of consulting as a career is that of “out sourcing”. For management, common sense dictates there is no reason to pay an employee a full time wage when the employee’s area of expertise is only required occasionally. It is much more cost effective to call in a specialty consultant or problem solving expert only when his or her particular expert advice is required.

HOME-BASED FREELANCERS

A *freelancer*, is a bit different than a consultant. A freelancer is simply a person who works independently in a specialized field by the hour, day, or job and usually for multiple employers. Whereas many consultants (such as a computer programmer) may often work at their employer’s business address, a freelancer will usually work from home or a private office.

BUSINESS DEVELOPMENT OFFICERS

In the factoring industry, firms will typically employ several in-house *business development officers* or BDOs. In fact, large factoring firms may have many such BDOs located in dozens of large cities nationwide. These individuals are usually paid through a salary / bonus arrangement based on their productivity and are true employees of the factoring firm. They do not broker or send business anywhere else unless it is pre-approved by their full time factor / employer.

So in the business of factoring, what are you? Well, you are a consultant to your client, the small business owner, who requires your expert sage advice on how to finance his business. But to your factor, you are a valued freelancer or independent broker who will be compensated for referrals on a deal-by-deal basis through a very, very attractive commission arrangement.

VERY ATTRACTIVE COMMISSION ARRANGEMENT

Commercial Finance Consultants

The term "factoring broker" is exactly what the name implies. It includes those brokers that practice in the factoring side of the industry and provide expert referral services when business owners require assistance in accessing some form of accounts receivable finance. Most often, the need for such expert referral service comes into play when a small business owner is turned down for a bank loan and simply does not know where else to turn for a ready financing alternative.

In some cases, solving this problem just encompasses a simple referral by the broker to a more accommodative bank. More often than not, however, it will probably involve arranging some form of alternative commercial finance solution such as factoring or asset-based lending. And here, of course, is where a knowledgeable broker / consultant is often needed since such financing options, and how to access their providers, are little known to the average small business owner.

LITTLE KNOWN TO THE AVERAGE BUSINESS OWNER

For some successful industry freelancers, the factoring product is simply not enough. This special group of brokers will expand their areas of financing knowledge and product expertise to the point where they are true small business financing experts. They are a highly prized and select group of independent freelance individuals providing small business owners with a cornucopia of financial services over an expansive array of product areas. Such professionals, referred to as CFCs or *commercial finance consultants,* will be able to provide ready sources of finance for accounts receivable, inventory, purchase orders, equipment, and virtually every other type of business asset which requires periodic financing. In some cases, they may even delve into the very difficult and mysterious areas of angel investing and professional venture capital.

COMMERCIAL FINANCE CONSULTANTS

So on one end of the group or spectrum of industry freelancers, you have factoring brokers who will focus their practice predominantly in one product area, commercial accounts receivable factoring. On the other end, you will find some career industry participants who have developed a level of expertise much more broad and diverse. It will include asset-based lending, equipment leasing, merchant cash advances, SBA lending, export trade finance, and the many other niche areas of business finance found throughout the asset-based finance industry.

It is important to note that in most instances, industry CFCs initially launch their career with a primary focus on the factoring product. Over time, they slowly build on that factoring expertise and expand their product lines to include the many other methods of business finance found in the asset-based finance community of lenders.

AUGMENTING THE INCOME FROM A CURRENT PROFESSION

Augmenting a Current Profession

So as you now know, factoring brokers have many opportunities to expand their businesses by gaining additional product knowledge and education. But there is also another industry group. Sourcing factoring solutions to small business owners also offers many professional services practitioners with a perfect opportunity to augment and subsidize the income they receive from a current vocation simply by adding a powerful new earnings resource. For example, bookkeepers, tax preparers, and other accounting professionals can add factoring as a new service area designed to assist their struggling small business accounting clients in need of cash flow or working capital solutions. Attorneys, practicing in the area of business law, can add the power of factoring as a financing method for assisting clients in need of quick working capital prior to or shortly after a reorganization bankruptcy filing (known as DIP financing). Savvy business brokers who learn of the power of factoring, can use this financial tool to solve problems related to accounts receivable value when a small business is sold to new owner.

Areas of Expanded Knowledge

For those individuals in search of an exciting new full-time career or even a part-time home-based business, the brokering of factoring related transactions, as well as the many other types of industry commercial finance products, provides an extraordinary opportunity to enter a truly unique vocation with earnings potential gauged very exceptional by any measure.

EXCEPTIONAL EARNINGS POTENTIAL

As an industry broker / consultant, your in-demand small business financial services help provide entrepreneurs with the ready capital they require to operate and grow their businesses successfully, while at the same time, earning you attractive fee and commission income. And as mentioned, though such "brokering" of factoring solutions is well practiced in Europe, this is a consulting career path which is relatively unknown in the U.S. and where the only real competition you will experience is from the lenders themselves.

Don't, however, take the decision to enter the industry lightly. Success as a broker in factoring and alternative commercial finance is far from guaranteed. To enjoy the exceptional income and many other benefits associated with this area of financial consulting, you will need to study, learn, and develop the considerable factoring product knowledge required to perform your services.

Other than factoring, there are several additional product areas which should be immediately recognized as "core products" for freelance brokers. These are products you will also need to quickly develop a working knowledge of. They include:

ADDITIONAL CORE PRODUCT AREAS

- **ASSET-BASED LENDING:** a facility created to provide a working capital loan (usually structured as a revolving line of credit) based on the value of accounts receivable, inventory, and equipment.
- **PURCHASE ORDER FINANCE:** financing, usually in the form of a letter of credit, utilized to purchase or manufacture goods required to fill a valid, large order from a creditworthy customer.
- **MERCHANT CASH ADVANCE:** an advance of lump sum cash to a business based on receiving a percentage of future credit card or over the counter sales receipts.

So even if you choose to limit your business to just factoring, you will immediately find the need for some additional basic alternative commercial finance product knowledge. For example, your regular day-to-day consulting business operations will require that you understand:

- which financing problems can easily be solved by factoring and which cannot.
- the differences between factoring, asset-based lending, and purchase order finance.
- the various specialized areas of factoring (i.e. construction factoring, freight bill factoring, agricultural factoring, government receivables factoring, DIP factoring, etc.) and where to locate those particular factors providing these specialized niche services.
- how to qualify prospective business owners for factoring, be able to recognize conditions which are "deal breakers", and be aware of the sources of remedy for such occasional problems.

Can You Do This Business?

One of the first questions that runs through anyone's mind as they explore a new business or career opportunity is, *can I do this?* The normal answer to such a question is simply, *I don't know.* In gauging your ability to succeed on a career level, a lot rides on two important considerations:

- What *soft skills* do you bring to the table as you begin.
- If your *soft skills* are weak, are you willing to spend the necessary time and energy developing them.

And so the *"I don't know"* answer is certainly correct. Anyone can learn the nuts and bolts of factoring. But developing marketing savvy is different and a great deal will depend on the soft skills you've come armed with or can develop for marketing your business.

But even that may be just a little too simplistic when it comes to brokering factoring transactions. Its just not that easy to say yes or no and here's why. (see case study next page)

Millie Stubblefield

Factoring Broker

Millie Stubblefield was a receptionist at a local bank in Lake Mount City, KY. As a bank employee she belonged to the local Chamber of Commerce and would periodically refer those she met socially at the Chamber to the bank for loans.

One day, she was pleasantly surprised to see a new Chamber acquaintance walk in the bank to apply for a business loan. The business owner had previously told her that his company, a condominium maintenance provider, was having some cash flow trouble and unless he could get a loan, he might have to lay off some employees and downsize a bit. Millie told him to stop by the bank and they would see what they could do.

Mille introduced the business owner to one of the bank's loan officers but unfortunately, there was little help the bank could provide. The business owner had poor credit and no collateral for a loan. The problem he was having was one of cash flow caused by his slow paying customers (management companies) which were taking 60 days or longer to pay for his services. As the business owner was leaving, Millie stopped him and gave him a phone number to call. It was the number of a local factor who had made a factoring presentation to the bank's employees earlier in the year. Millie thought factoring just might be the solution for this business.

Later that day the business owner placed a call to the factor who immediately set up an appointment. It was clear that the business owner's cash flow problem was being caused by the slow paying management companies and that factoring would provide a ready solution. Each week, the factor would purchase the maintenance company's invoices with an up-front 80% advance. The factor would then wait to get paid in 60 days. Once paid, the factor would remit the remaining 20% less a 5% fee for its factoring services.

With over a 40% profit margin, the maintenance company's owner could easily absorb the factoring costs. He would now receive payment within hours of completing his work and his customers could still enjoy their 60 day payment terms...all because of factoring.

For Millie, there was an added bonus. Although she did nothing more than provide a phone number that resulted in a new client being added to the factor's portfolio, she was now the *broker of record* for that referral and would be entitled to a monthly commission check. The maintenance company was generating about $100,000 in billings each month. As the broker of record Millie would receive 15% of the factoring fees earned or about $750 per month. Additionally, she would receive those checks for the life of the account which is typically 5 years or longer. This could represent a total income package of over $45,000...FOR ONE REFERRAL!

Broker commissions paid in the factoring industry are residual, meaning they will be paid month after month, year after year, so long as the company referred continues to utilize the services of the factor. It is not unusual for a typical client / factor relationship to last 4 years, 5 years, 6 years or even longer. In the previous case study, a five year relationship yielded roughly $45,000 in total commission payments to Millie, the broker of record.

RIGHT PLACE
RIGHT TIME
RIGHT KNOWLEDGE

So if you're asking yourself the question, *can I do this business,* the answer is still, *I don't know.* But after seeing the previous example of a brokered factoring transaction, one which was simply the result of being in the right place, at the right time, armed with the right knowledge, and which can easily result in total earnings of $30,000, $40,000, or even $50,000 to the referring broker over time, the NEW question is or at least should be:

Can I afford NOT to invest the time in acquiring this kind of "RIGHT KNOWLEDGE"?

Factoring Consultant Characteristics

Factoring brokers come in a wide range of styles and flavors. This is a very flexible industry that can accommodate part-time occasional practitioners, full-time careers seekers, and everything in between. But as we said before, almost no one entering the industry's brokering community actually comes fully equipped from day one to excel. The vast majority choosing to embark on this journey will need to acquire industry specific product knowledge, develop or hone certain marketing skills, and probably both.

EXCEPTIONAL REWARD

Regardless of the amount of preparation required, the reward for doing such personal "upgrading" is exceptional. Those with the intention of participating only occasionally and sending their referrals to a factor just once or twice a year, can probably do so by simply investing a little time in learning a bit more about the factoring process. In fact, most can easily acquire the necessary product knowledge just by reading this guide. After doing so, they will be able to speak intelligently about how factoring works and get an occasional client. The requirements to enter the industry with full-time career intentions, however, are quite a bit different.

Career factoring brokers and commercial finance consultants tend to be derived from the determined "opportunist" style of today's entrepreneurs. They are "mobile creatives", drawn to those business opportunities where residual and renewable income is a feature. Although they may not initially have the required skillsets to successfully commence a particular venture, they are very willing to devote the time to develop and learn them to achieve success.

A SUIT AND TIE BUSINESS

Career oriented industry entrants will find this enterprise to be very much a suit and tie business. Many will have to embark on a journey of personal upgrading to "remanufacture" themselves as true consulting professionals.

Normal days for career brokers will be spent networking with local sources of referral such as loan officers, accounting professionals, and others. There will be meetings with business owners, workshops to hold, speaking engagements, and luncheons and club meetings where knowledge can be shared. Career brokers will create lead-generating marketing campaigns, implement those campaigns, and then prospect the leads generated through telephone follow up. They will create and distribute informative small business newsletters, hold periodic guest speaker teleconferences, develop irresistible offers, manage a consultant website, and create and update prospect databases and lists.

FOR SELF-STARTING HARD WORKERS

So as you now may be realizing, full-time participation in this business is just not that simple. It is a career for self-starting, hard workers and one to be taken very seriously. Those viewing the industry as the next get rich quick and easy scheme, characterized by minimal work, are in for quite a rude awakening.

Productive brokers who can generate quality clients are always in great demand by industry factors since they represent a valuable productivity resource which gets compensated only on performance. In fact, virtually every factor's website contains some page or area strictly devoted to soliciting business from freelance independent brokers. Don't believe it? Just try this.

With the help of your favorite search engine, take a moment to visit any factor's website. They are very easy to find. If you're having trouble though, just visit www.dmoz.org. From DMOZ's site map, select:

DMOZ.ORG

BUSINESS > FINANCIAL SERVICES > FACTORING

You will find a large list of factors displayed. Click on any link to visit that factor's website. Somewhere on the site, within easy access, you will see a link to an area or page entitled *Brokers, Referrals, Partners*, or something similar. Those pages will explain that particular factor's broker program, commission payout arrangements, and often much more. Industry statistics reveal over one half of all new factoring clients generated each year are the result of a referral and many of those referrals are sourced from successful independent industry factoring brokers. All factors eagerly solicit independent brokers and especially those with proven track records when it comes to generating quality leads.

Getting Started

Factoring 101: A Broker's Guide is a very comprehensive how-to manual for new industry entrants and will likely provide you with all the training you will require to start your journey and begin earning industry commission income. Below are a few "helps and hints" to make sure you get the most from this training guide.

COVER-TO-COVER TWICE

- Read this training guide cover-to-cover at least twice. Avoid using it solely as a reference.
- Answer the questions at the end of each chapter. We have placed the answers to all questions at the back of the guide.

TAKE THE PROFICIENCY EXAM

- Take the *IACFB Proficiency Exam* located in the *Learning Lab* after completing the training. One of the greatest fears new consultants have is that they DO NOT KNOW ENOUGH and will be embarrassed or exposed as a novice. If you can score a 85% or higher on our *Proficiency Exam*, you have learned more than what you need to launch your new business.

Chapter 1 Quiz

TAKE THE QUIZ

1. Nearly___________ million Americans have left the American labor force as of this writing.
   - A. 35
   - B. 52
   - C. 94
   - D. 106

2. A factoring broker is someone who periodically refers a business owner to a factor or lender and______________
   - A. earns a commission
   - B. becomes broker of record
   - C. is an independent contractor
   - D. all of the above

3. Most factors will have inside _________ for business development.
   - A. account executives
   - B. business development officers
   - C. BDOs
   - D. both B & C

4. A "CORE" product used by small business to finance accounts receivable, inventory, and equipment is _____________________
   - A. merchant cash advance
   - B. factoring
   - C. purchase order finance
   - D. asset-based lending

5. As the "*Broker of Record*" on a referred factoring client, you will normally earn ______ percent of the factoring fees for the life of the account.
   - A. 5
   - B. 10
   - C. 15
   - D. 25

ANSWERS TO THESE AND OTHER QUESTIONS CAN BE FOUND IN THE BACK OF THE GUIDE

LEARNING TRANSACTIONAL BASICS

The Basic Concepts of Factoring

As we have already discussed, consultants are utilized throughout various industries as a result of having a specialized expertise or unique knowledge of a product, service, concept, etc. As a new factoring broker, you will need to gain such expertise in factoring and several related areas of asset-based finance if you want to be a true professional. The more you understand about the industry and the more knowledge you accumulate, the more valuable you become to small business owners as well as to your important sources of referral such as bank lending officers and accounting professionals. In short, you need to know your stuff.

THE MORE YOU LEARN, THE MORE VALUABLE YOU BECOME

Fortunately, factoring is a relatively simple form of commercial finance and once you grasp a few basic concepts, your product knowledge will expand fairly rapidly. Factoring is really just a financing method used by businesses to obtain cash. Factoring is considered a type of *asset-based finance* (ABF) along with asset-based lending, equipment leasing, inventory finance and purchase order finance among others.

A RELATIVELY SIMPLE FORM OF COMMERCIAL FINANCE

Asset-Based Finance is pretty much exactly what it sounds like, a method of financing based on the assets of a business. In the vast majority of instances, however, asset-based finance will involve only the "primary" assets found in almost any business entity. Primary assets include:

- **accounts receivable**
- **inventory**
- **equipment**

MORE OFTEN FINANCED WITH AN AMORTIZED LOAN STRUCTURE

Real estate, also an often found business asset, is usually excluded in discussions of asset-based finance since real property is more typically financed in a separate transaction utilizing long-term amortized loan structures.

DYNAMIC COLLATERALS

Asset-based finance often tends to deal with the financing complexities associated with *collaterals* which are dynamic and whose value and location can change rapidly. An example would be business inventory, which is constantly being decreased as sales are produced and increased as replacement goods are purchased or manufactured. Real estate, on the other hand, tends to be more static in nature and an asset whose value (and location) is always easy to ascertain and monitor by the lender.

Important Factoring Terminology

All industries tend to have a certain amount of industry-specific jargon associated with day-to-day operations and the factoring industry is no different. To follow are some basic (but important) terms you should become very familiar with as an industry broker.

- **ADVANCE:** an initial disbursement of funds by a factor to the seller upon purchased invoices. (Typically 80 percent)
- **ACCOUNT:** an account receivable or simply, an invoice
- **ACCOUNT DEBTOR:** another name for the customer or the party obligated to make payment upon an account

- **ASSIGNMENT:** the assignment of ownership to a factor of the invoices and rights involving such invoices
- **CLIENT:** the business that is selling its invoices to a factor
- **CUSTOMER:** a more common term for the account debtor obligated to make payment on an invoice
- **DISCOUNT:** the fee amount charged over the period an account is outstanding for the factor's service (the "Factoring Fee")
- **NON-RECOURSE:** a factoring arrangement in which the factor assumes the non-payment risks associated with the bankruptcy or insolvency of a customer
- **NOTIFICATION of ASSIGMENT:** a notice sent to an account debtor regarding the assignment of ownership in the accounts of a business and rights to payment upon those accounts
- **RECOURSE:** a factoring arrangement where the factor has the right to charge-back purchased invoice amounts to the client if payment is not received from the account debtor within a specific period of time (usually 90 days)
- **RESERVE:** the percentage of the face value of an invoice not advanced and used to secure the factor against trade disputes, reduced invoice payment, or non-payment
- **RESERVE DISTRIBUTION:** commonly called a "rebate", is the periodic payment to the client of the excess reserve held by the factor

NOTES

SENT TO ACCOUNT DEBTORS

Factoring Traditionally Defined

As mentioned, factoring is a relatively simple form of commercial asset-based finance and is traditionally defined as:

A method of commercial finance in which a business (known as the client) periodically sells its accounts receivable or invoices to a specialized finance company (known as the factor). Such "factored" invoices are purchased by the factor at a discount to their face value.

A RELATIVELY SIMPLE FORM OF COMMERCIAL FINANCE

A Simple Discount Transaction

So factoring is simply a discount transaction where an asset of a business is purchased at a small discount to its face value. In the case of factoring, the asset is accounts receivable. The discount or fee charged to the seller for such services depends on many things such as:

- The size of the invoices to be purchased (dollar value)
- The total dollar amount sold weekly or periodically
- The creditworthiness of the account debtor (customer)
- Type of transaction (recourse or non-recourse)
- Other risks (international, governmental, perishable goods, etc.)

Say a client generates $5,000 in invoices each week but each invoice is only $250 (20 invoices). Let's also say that those invoices represent sales to customers who might be best described as very small "mom and pop" operations. The discount charged by the factor would be higher than average for such a transaction due to the amount of additional work necessary for processing such small accounts as well as the risks.

Conversely, if a client generates one single $5,000 invoice per week representing a sale to a single, large, creditworthy customer, the discount would be less than average reflecting the minimal amount of work needed to process the transaction and the minimal amount of credit risk.

REVIEWING
CASE STUDIES

Case Studies

Before we delve any deeper into factoring, its time to look at a few real live examples. One of the best ways for new brokers to learn about any new concept is through *case studies.* For our purposes, the case studies featured in this guide will provide you with some true life examples of how factoring has been used to solve particular problems of various small businesses. All are based on real client examples, although the names of clients and customers have obviously been changed. The following three case studies are very typical examples of what you will run into as a freelance factoring consultant.

Lester Thornton started *Lester's Security Plus* on a shoestring budget in 2009 initially financed with a $20,000 Home Equity Line of Credit (HELOC). *Lester's Security Plus* primarily provides guards for local gated communities and has gained a good reputation among the real estate management companies in the area.

Last year, Lester received an offer to provide gate guards for four existing communities from a local management company. The management company, *ManageCo*, was replacing their previous service and wanted Lester to provide a bid which he did. Lester was awarded the new contract but immediately found he had a problem. The new management company was a very slow payer on its invoices, taking nearly 60 days in fact. Lester had always paid his guards weekly which meant he would have to fund the payroll for the new guards for roughly nine weeks before the first check came in from *ManageCo*. With guards required around the clock at all four facilities, Lester would be making payroll for the new guards of over $6,000 per week (168 hours per week x $9 per hour x 4 facilities). He would need to make that payroll for 9 weeks or come out of pocket nearly $55,000 before he received payment on the first invoice.

Lester simply did not have that kind of money available and unfortunately, had no ability to borrow more using his HELOC. He did, however, remember meeting a small business finance specialist named Jerry Goggins at a *Chamber of Commerce* meetup. Jerry and Lester had discussed the possible use of something called *factoring* to finance *Security Plus* if it ever became necessary. It had suddenly become necessary, and Lester made a call to Jerry.

After the call, Lester and Jerry met for lunch to discuss financing and Jerry quickly recognized that factoring would solve this problem. Jerry worked with a factor that specialized in service sector finance and he knew the factor's flat fee rate was about 5-6 percent for 60 days. Lester had over a 50% profit margin on his services so he could easily absorb the factoring fee. After lunch, Jerry went back to Lester's office and they made a quick call to the factor who was available to discuss a factoring arrangement.

On the call, the factor asked about the business loan and was assured it was secured by Lester's home and not the business assets. The factor gave Lester a tentative rate of 1.25% for 15 days which meant the 60 day payment would only be charged 5% but it also meant Lester could factor all of his other receivables, which were usually paid in 30 days or less. All in all, *Security Plus* would be financing about $120,000 per month.

Lester's finance problem was solved. Jerry, because of his relationship with Lester, now would earn a monthly referral commission from the factor. **FACTORING COMMISSION EARNINGS: $400 - $600 per month.**

Jackson Sprokett, better known as "Cactus Jack", was a metal fabricator specializing in custom fenders and fuel tanks for motorcycles. He started *Cactus Jack's Custom Tanks* in 2001.

Jack was an expert in the use of an English wheel, a special tool used to shape sheet metal, and had become well known in the custom bike community after being featured in a well read biker magazine with national circulation. Business had picked up dramatically after the article and his shop was always busy, although primarily for one-off fabrications for individuals.

Shortly after the featured article, Jack was contacted by a regional motorcycle custom parts supplier about supplying an exclusive line of "Cactus Jack" fenders and tanks. The supplier had 37 stores and would be carrying "Cactus Jack" inventory in each along with special order options. They estimated that would need about $3,000 in tank and fender inventory in each store monthly or a little over $110,000. Terms of sale would be 45 day net which gave the supplier ample time to sell the goods prior to payment.

Jack was delighted with the prospective order but his was a small custom shop and he would need to hire at least one additional aluminum fabricator and one gas welder skilled at thin gauge aluminum welding. Neither would come cheap. He would need some payroll financing because of the 45 day terms of payment required by the supplier.

Jack's brother had a local janitorial service that had been using something called *factoring* for years to finance its payroll and he wondered if factoring would also work for him. He called his brother and got the phone number of the factor and made a call.

On the call, Jack explained the opportunity to his brother's factor who quickly looked at the credit rating of the parts supplier. It was excellent and would be enough to provide a credit limit of $100,000 so that Jack could finance 100% of the supplier's invoices. Jack had no bank financing in place so the factor could enjoy a secured 1st lien position in accounts receivable which is always required in factoring.

The factor assigned an account executive to the account and the Jack received a factoring contract (called a Master Purchase and Sales Agreement) via overnight courier. He quickly executed the contract and returned it to the factor. *Cactus Jack's Custom Tanks* could now comfortably hire the two new employees needed to fabricate the quantity of tanks and fenders needed to meet the new orders.

FACTORING COMMISSION EARNINGS (Had one been involved): $750 - $1,000 per month.

Ziggy's

Welding Specialties

Onsite Equipment Repair

Dieter Ziggens started *Ziggy's Welding Specialties* in Tampa, FL to provide onsite welding services for construction equipment. Ziggy's has grown rapidly since opening in 1999 and currently has two (2) mobile welding trucks to provide services to local contractors.

Dieter Ziggens was pleasantly surprised to receive a call one day from a national steel building contractor in need of mobile services. The contractor was beginning operations in Florida and would need an onsite mobile operator for at least the next 24 months to service new steel building being erected. The hourly fee offered was exceptional, however Ziggens would need to submit a single invoice each month for all work completed during that calendar month. The invoice would then be paid within 30 days. That meant Ziggens may have to wait as long as 60 days to be paid on some work. Additionally, Ziggens would likely need to outfit another vehicle just to handle the steel building contractor's additional business which was estimated to be $100,000 per month. Ziggens was already billing about $150,000 per month with local contractors who paid in 30 days or less. This new business meant billings of roughly $250,000 and Ziggens decided to talk to his banker about a loan.

At a meeting with a loan officer at his local bank, Ziggens was given the unfortunate news that the bank would not be able to help since they only offered real estate financing and not asset-based loans. The loan officer said it really sounded like Ziggens could use something called *factoring* and he provided Ziggens with the name of a local consultant he had referred business to before that specialized in *factoring* for the construction industry.

After leaving the bank a little worried, Ziggens called the consultant who met with him that afternoon. The consultant agreed that so long as the steel building contractor's credit was good, factoring would do the job and a conference call was set up with a factor for later that afternoon.

On the call, the factor quickly researched the credit of the steel building contractor and found it was good. He also requested an accounts receivable aging report to pull credit on Ziggens' other clients. Once received, he would provide Ziggens with a "Terms Sheet" with pricing.

Within 48 hours, *Ziggy's Welding Specialties* was provided with a $250,000 factoring credit facility. Ziggens would now be factoring all of his invoices and the factor would act as his accounts receivable finance and management team. At an average discount rate for services of 4%, the factoring fees would be little more than accepting a credit card and Ziggens could now hire additional staff as well as purchase and outfit an additional vehicle. **FACTORING COMMISSION EARNINGS: $1,000 - $1,500 per month.**

Factoring vs. Lending

FACTORING IS NEVER A LOAN

Factoring is easily distinguished from the more common methods of business finance provided by most banks in that true *factoring* is never a structured as a *loan*, but rather as a *purchase and sale* transaction. Also, since factoring only relates to invoiced sales, it is strictly a method of financing business-to-business or B2B transactions. It is very important for brokers to understand that factoring is not used to directly finance retail consumer transactions. Understandably, when immediate payment is received by cash or credit card at time of sale, there is no invoice or extension of payment terms and factoring would be, by definition, unnecessary.

FACTORING INVOLVES THREE PARTIES

Rather than just the two parties commonly involved in an normal business loan (the borrower and lender), there are always three parties involved in any factoring transaction. These are the:

- **client**...the seller of the invoices
- **factor**...the buyer of the invoices
- **account debtor**...the client's customer obligated to make payment upon the invoice

ALWAYS USED TO FINANCE TERMS OF PAYMENT

Working capital generated by factoring business accounts receivable can be used for hundreds of purposes such as buying equipment, paying suppliers, purchasing inventory, etc. The factoring process itself is only utilized for one thing, however, and that is to provide a method of financing extended *terms of payment* for customers. Financing sales made to customers on credit terms is an essential component of good cash flow management. Factoring provides that financing solution for small businesses worldwide.

The use of the term "factoring" has grown over the years to include any financial transaction which involves *discounting*. For example, buyers of *structured settlements* are said to "factor" the annuitized settlement payment streams when making lump sum annuity purchases. Credit card companies are said to be factors due to the discount charged to the merchant for guarantying the payment made by a consumer. For our purposes, however, we will limit the discussion of factoring and the presentation in this guide to the simple discounted purchase of business trade receivables.

Understanding Terms of Payment

Because factoring tends to be used solely to finance the terms of payment extended by a business to its customers, brokers should become very familiar with this concept and why the granting of terms of payment is so important (and often problematic) to small business.

In everyday business transactions, terms of payment are simply the conditions set forth regarding payment for delivered goods or services. When providing over-the-counter retail products or services, terms of payment are NOW, by immediate cash or credit card! In invoiced sales transactions between businesses (B2B), extended terms of payment are granted and will set forth the amount of time the customer has to remit payment for the goods or services purchased.

In B2B commerce, common terms of payment granted to buyers are 10, 15, or 30 days. In large international transactions, terms of payment can become much more complex and may include payment "conditions" such as trade documents processing or the posting of a *trade* or *standby letter of credit* guarantying timely payment to the seller. Terms of payment granted to customers may also feature discount offers for fast payment. For example, terms granted to a buyer of “two percent net 30” means the seller can discount the amount due upon the invoice by 2% of the balance if the payment is remitted in less than 30 days.

TERMS OF PAYMENT MAY FEATURE DISCOUNTS

There are many reasons for a small business to grant terms of payment to its customers. In some cases, it is simply because the customer is a large, creditworthy company that demands them. The small business must agree to grant terms of payment so it can receive the order. In other instances, extended payment terms are granted to keep existing customers happy and to maintain competitiveness in the marketplace. Attractive terms of payment can also be used to “woo” customers away from more established competition.

LARGE, CREDITWORTHY CUSTOMERS DEMAND TERMS OF PAYMENT

But, no matter what the reason for granting terms, the result is always the same. The small business owner has suddenly found himself in the position of *financier* and is, in fact, financing a customer's business by granting credit in the form of payment terms.

Unfortunately, by helping to finance the enterprises of customers, a business owner may also be creating a serious cash flow problem for his own company. All of those attractive payment terms granted to customers can suddenly add up and an owner may find himself chasing the checks of late paying customers just to make sure the cash is available for his own weekly employee payroll.

ONLY TWO WAYS TO ATTACK TERMS OF PAYMENT PROBLEMS

For businesses with limited working capital, there are really only two ways to attack the terms of payment issue:

1. **Stop extending credit to customers (which may result in losing existing customers and may cripple the ability to attract new ones).**
2. **Arrange for a method of financing accounts receivable.**

Factoring, and several other forms of asset-based finance, are specifically designed to remedy such cash flow problems associated with invoiced sales. For smaller, non-bankable companies with a limited credit history, factoring is often the only readily available financing choice. That is because of how factoring is structured, as a "purchase and sale" transaction and not as a loan.

FACTORING WORKS ON "OPC" OR OTHER PEOPLE'S CREDIT

Almost everyone has heard of the term OPM or "other people's money". Factoring is a readily accessible cash flow solution for very young companies with minimal financial history because it operates on OPC or "other people's credit". Unlike a traditional bank loan where the bank looks at the borrower's creditworthiness, with factoring, the business owner's credit (or lack thereof) is of a secondary consideration. When underwriting a new client, the factor is much more interested in the credit history of the business owner's customers, the ones who will actually be making payment on the purchased invoices.

Invoices & Eligibility

NOTES

Factors are not buyers of delinquent debt or invoices with perceived payment problems. While this concept may seem relatively straight forward, it actually is not. This is because not all invoices are created equal and certain types of invoices, with conditions for payment, can disqualify them for purchase by a factor, such as...

- **CONSIGNMENT INVOICES:** Goods sent to a customer on *consignment* are goods which the customer will use its best efforts to sell but will not actually purchase. In the event the goods do not sell, they are returned to the manufacturer / distributor and payment is only made upon the goods actually sold.
- **PRE-SHIP INVOICES:** This is not a true invoice since the service has yet to be performed by the client or the goods have yet to be shipped and delivered.

PRE-SHIP INVOICES

- **GOVERNMENT RECEIVABLES:** Invoices payable by cities, states, or the federal government will sometimes not be acceptable to a factor. This is usually due to the factor's inability to properly "notice" the governmental entity regarding payment. Fortunately, there are specialized "niche" factors that routinely handle such difficult transactions involving governmental entities.
- **OVER 90 DAY RECEIVABLES:** Factors only purchase invoices payable under normal terms (under 90 days). Factors are NOT bill collectors and do not purchase delinquent debt and questionable invoices.
- **INVOICES SUBJECT TO LIEN:** Invoices which are subject to a *mechanics lien* represent a minefield when purchased since payments can be subject to "priming" or having someone jump ahead of the factor for payment. This is very common when factoring general contractors and can also occur when factoring certain food producers.

MECHANIC'S LIENS

- **CONTRAS:** A *contra* occurs when a factor's client and an account debtor sell goods or services to each other and subsequently exchange invoices. When a contra exists, there is always the risk that both parties will agree to simply offset or cancel invoice payments due.

- **CONTINGENT INVOICES:** A *contingent* invoice is one whose payment is dependent upon the performance of another service. For example, the payment upon an invoice for computer equipment and hardware may be contingent upon the seller's proper installation of that equipment and hardware.
- **FOREIGN ACCOUNTS:** Foreign accounts are those payable by a business in a foreign country. When dealing with foreign accounts, even though a factor may be able to perfect a foreign security interest, the problems which can occur regarding actual collection often make such foreign accounts undesirable.
- **POOR CREDIT QUALITY:** Some receivables are simply ineligible for purchase due to the poor credit quality of the customer.

The Bottom Line

MARKETING WITH DELINQUENT DEBT

As you begin to generate your first leads from your marketing efforts, you will probably get responses from quite a few small businesses with accounts that are "problem" accounts. Many small business owners carrying delinquent debt would love to sell some to a factor and recoup 80 percent of their money. Very few factors, however, are in the delinquent debt business. Brokers can earn commission income, however, by placing delinquent debt with debt collectors. In fact, making cold calls to business owners regarding delinquent debt can often lead to a conversation about financing their regular trade invoices through factoring or asset-based loans.

Another type of problem every broker is sure to run into is that of pre-ship invoices or invoices where the work has yet to be done or where the goods have not been delivered. For example, a janitorial service may actually invoice a client on the first day of the billing month for cleaning services which WILL BE performed over the next 4-5 weeks. This is *pre-billing* and such invoices cannot be purchased by a factor until the work is completed. Some factors, however, have gotten creative regarding client advances based upon monthly pre-billing by only releasing a portion of the advance, week by week, as the work is actually completed.

8 Reasons to Employ Factoring

The need for factoring is usually the result of an inability of a business to access traditional bank loans or lines of credit, a trait that is of even greater importance in today's challenging economy. So it is really no surprise that modern business owners are becoming increasingly more aware of factoring as a ready form of alternative commercial finance and one which can be employed quickly in times of cash flow and working capital crisis.

From a technical financing standpoint, and as you now understand, factoring is only utilized to address the cash flow problems caused by extending terms of payment to customers and the working capital shortfalls such extensions can ultimately create. Shortages of working capital can result in serious problems for business owners who will then seek out some financial option as a remedy. Problems associated with working capital shortages which can drive a small business to seek factoring include:

PROBLEMS OF CASH FLOW CAUSED BY TERMS OF PAYMENT

- ⇒ **PAYROLL:** Shortages of cash when payroll is due are by far the most common reason for a business to seek out the services of a factor.
- ⇒ **SUPPLIER PAYABLES:** Making timely payments to suppliers or also being able to take discounts for early supplier payments.
- ⇒ **TAX OBLIGATIONS:** Especially payments associated with employee 941 payroll taxes.
- ⇒ **EQUIPMENT:** Raising cash through the sale of invoices to purchase equipment when leasing is not an option.
- ⇒ **INVENTORY:** Purchasing inventory when other forms of lending are not available.
- ⇒ **MARKETING:** Expanding and increasing marketing operations.
- ⇒ **EXPANSION:** Raising capital to enter new markets, buy out a competitor, or other forms of business expansion.
- ⇒ **INVESTMENT OPPORTUNITIES:** Raising cash for an investment opportunity such as buying a building or purchasing an additional franchise.

Snagmasters

Mag Force

TURBO SINKERS

Avid bass fishing pro, Bill "Sawtooth" Snagmaster is well known around the pro bass fishing circuit as a designer of the world's finest turbo sinkers. Due to popular demand throughout the pro bass circuit, he began producing his always-in-demand *Mag Force Deluxe Turbo Sinkers* out of his garage and selling them to other pro fisherman.

One day, to Bill's surprise, he received a call from a major fishing equipment retailer, *Batfish Bobbers,* wanting to order 50,000 turbo sinkers per month (in various popular colors) for its retail chain. *Bobbers* would pay 50 cents per sinker ($25,000 per month) and the terms of payment required by *Bobbers* was 60 days.

In spite of running his business from his garage, Bill felt he could easily meet the $25,000 monthly order size and he currently had over 50,000 sinkers in inventory....enough to meet the first order. But, there was a small problem. While he had plenty of inventory for the first order, he would need to order bulk lead, special sinker ferrules, and waterproof color dye for the subsequent two sinker orders if he was to meet the required shipping dates. He estimated the cost of these raw materials at about $10,000 per order and this was money Bill simply did not have at hand.

Fortunately for Bill, one of his closest fishing buddies and *Mag Force Turbo Sinker* fan, Pete, was a freelance factoring broker who worked the fishing circuit looking for opportunities just like this. Pete had already talked to Bill about financing in case he ever landed a big order so it was no surprise when Bill called and explained the situation. Pete immediately concluded that a small factoring arrangement was all Bill needed and quickly set up a conference call that very afternoon with a factor.

To begin the call, Pete made the introduction between Bill and the factor and within just a few minutes, the factor recognized the opportunity and had conditionally approved *Snagmaster Turbo Sinkers* for factoring. In addition, because of its excellent credit rating, *Batfish Bobbers* was approved with a credit limit of $200,000 which gave Bill plenty of financial room to increase shipments and order size if required.

ANALYSIS...ACCEPTED: This deal was accepted. Bill was provided with a factoring arrangement featuring an 80% advance, a fee rate of 2.5% for 30 days and just 4.5% total for 60 days. The 80% initial advance on the first invoice purchased provided *Snagmasters* with $20,000 in immediate funding (80% x $25,000 invoice) so Bill could comfortably order the raw materials for the next orders. More importantly, with the factoring arrangement now in place, Bill could easily handle what he felt would be new orders from other retailers which were competitors of *Batfish Bobbers.*

As the factoring broker of record, Pete earned a standard monthly referral fee of approximately $340.00 for every month Bill factors. **BROKER COMMISSION EARNINGS: $350-$400 per month** to start but may grow significantly as *Snagmasters* attracts new orders from other retailers and competitors of *Batfish Bobbers*.

Froggie's

Tennis Racquet Grips

Made With Real Italian Frog Hair

Froggie's Tennis Racquet Grips, Inc. is a manufacturer of custom frog hair replacement grips for tennis and racquetball racquets. Ron Ribbit, owner of Froggie's, sells to over 500 tennis equipment pro shops nationwide and has financed his business to date with an SBA loan of $150,000 which was used to purchase inventory.

Ribbit was approached by *Product Crammers*, an online / infomercial marketing company, which wanted to shoot several infomercials for *Froggie's Grips* and market the product through various late night televised merchants. *Product Crammers* estimated it would need about 10,000 grips at a wholesale cost of $10 per grip to fulfill the anticipated orders. This would amount to about $100,000 in new inventory.

Ron Ribbit has always wondered if his genuine frog hair grips could be sold using infomercials and told *Product Crammers* he was interested but would like more information regarding the transaction. Specifically, what would be the terms of payment and who would fulfill the orders as they come in. *Product Crammers* told him they would fulfill the orders and he would be paid in 30 days for the merchandise sold. Ribbit agreed to the transaction but told *Product Crammers* he would need to arrange for additional credit at his bank to purchase enough imported fine Italian frog hair to make the grips for an order this size.

Ribbit arranged an appointment with his loan officer at the bank to discuss accessing some additional credit. Unfortunately, his loan officer informed him that his line of credit was maxed out unless he could provide additional collateral, which he could not. The loan officer did, however, have an idea for Ribbit and suggested he contact a commercial factor to finance the receivables payable by *Product Crammers*. And, although the bank did have a collateral position secured by "All Assets" of *Froggie's Tennis Racquet Grips, Inc.* to secure the existing SBA loan, they would subordinate their senior lien holder status on all of the receivables payable by *OnlineCo* so the factor would have rights to collect payment on the purchased accounts.

Ribbit contacted a local factor suggested by his loan office and explained the deal to him. The factor immediately provided Ribbit with a conditional "Terms Sheet" outlining the factoring fees, advance rates, and financing requirements and subsequently created the factoring contract (Master Purchase and Sales Agreement) so the account could be established while due diligence was taking place.

ANALYSIS...DECLINED: While *Product Crammers'* credit was solid enough for the factor to provide the financing, another problem unfortunately surfaced during the due diligence process which was the payment arrangement set forth in the purchase order. Under the purchase arrangement, *Product Crammers* only agreed to pay for the number of grips actually sold during the infomercial promotion. The balance of the grips left unsold, would be returned to *Froggie's* and that amount deducted from the payment of the invoice. This arrangement made the transaction one of *consignment* and due to the uncertainty of receiving full payment on the purchased invoices, this particular transaction would be declined by the factor. **BROKER COMMISSION: 0**

The entire list of reasons for a business to utilize receivables finance and establish a factoring arrangement is fairly expansive. In most cases, however, savvy brokers know working capital shortages will tend to first appear when cash is in short supply for the timely payment of employee payroll.

MANY BROKERS FOCUS ON THE SERVICE SECTOR

As we will discuss in later chapters on marketing, one reason why experienced factoring brokers focus much of their business development efforts on payroll intensive, services related prospects such as staffing companies, guard services, janitorial services, landscaping companies, etc., is because of their typically large payroll responsibilities. These are businesses that tend to have an abundance of employees and sizable weekly or bi-weekly payrolls. For brokers, they can represent "low hanging fruit" for prospecting and as we will discuss later, such small service companies with an abundance of employees are a great place to start marketing.

Characteristics of a Typical Factoring Client

You can now better understand why terms of payment can cause cash shortages and also why a small business owner would look to factoring as a ready solution to such shortages. But now let's look at factoring from the another viewpoint, the factor's viewpoint. So, what characteristics make a business a good candidate for factoring?

WHAT MAKES A GOOD FACTORING CLIENT

Over the last 50 years, factoring has expanded rapidly in the U.S. and now touches hundreds of industries. Still, all business owners in every industry do not qualify for factoring. For industry brokers, being able to focus your marketing efforts and campaigns on those business types which will yield the best results and have the highest possibility of becoming commission-generating clients is important. The following are some common characteristics of an acceptable prospect, from the factor's (and broker's) perspective.

- **UNENCUMBERED INVOICES:** The factor must have a FIRST PRIORITY lien secured by the accounts receivable of the client. This means there can be no previous lender in place that has a prior right to invoices as a collateral.

- **BUSINESS TO BUSINESS (B2B) INVOICED SALES:** As a method of business finance, factoring only addresses one area, and that is the cash flow problems associated with granting terms of payment upon invoices. As such, only businesses that invoice to other businesses (B2B) for goods or services are eligible for factoring. Factoring, as a financial tool, MUST ALWAYS INVOLVE AN INVOICE. The goods must have already been delivered or the services already performed.

INVOICED SALES ONLY

- **ASSIGNABLE INVOICES:** Factors will require the ability to "notice" the customers of a client so they will make payment directly to the factor's address or lockbox and no longer to the client. For legal notification, this requires that the purchased invoices be "assignable".

  Notification is typically not a problem with any normal trade invoices. Assignment provisions, however, can become complex when dealing with federal or certain state or municipal governmental entities.

- **ACCEPTABLE PROFIT MARGINS:** Factors will look at profit margins before taking on a new client to ascertain whether the client has enough transactional profit to absorb the costs of factoring. Most factors will want to see at least a 15% profit margin. Very few small business owners operate below or near this level. You will find most service providers to be in the 30% or above and many manufactures in the 50%-100% range or even higher. Still some industries, such as agricultural growers (fruits and vegetables), can operate on very low profits.

- **FEDERAL TAX LIENS:** Prior to establishing a factoring relationship with a new client, the factor will search for existing *federal tax liens.* Federal tax liens usually involve unpaid 941 taxes (payroll). Federal tax liens are "super liens" and can *prime* or jump ahead of a lender's assignment rights. A factoring relationship cannot be established if there is an existing federal tax lien which cannot be satisfied, remedied or subordinated.

FEDERAL TAX LIENS JUMP AHEAD

SAVVY BROKERS LOOK FOR TAX LIEN PROBLEMS

SPOT FACTORING

NOTE: While an existing tax lien will often prohibit a financing relationship, there are several methods of dealing with such liens so a relationship can be established. These include:

- **paying off the tax arrearage out of the first financing**
- **obtaining a lien subordination from the IRS**
- **making payments to IRS under an existing payment plan**

Many experienced, well "seasoned" brokers will look for businesses suffering from tax liens and prospect them with a possible solution to their tax problem. In virtually all cases, a business owner with back taxes owing would much rather deal with a factor than with the IRS.

- **CONTINUOUS NEED FOR FACTORING SERVICES:** A business seeking the services of a factor should exhibit a continuous need for financing. In fact, most factors will require a minimum of a one year contract with a specified minimum acceptable amount of invoices submitted for factoring each month. Business owners that have only a periodic or a very occasional need for factoring will find it much more difficult to attract a suitable provider.

While most factors are relatively strict regarding the continuous need provision, exceptions are routinely made for those clients requiring only "seasonal" factoring. This is very common for certain companies whose business spikes markedly during the holiday season when sales to large, creditworthy retailers increase significantly for just a few short months.

Some businesses will not require factoring on an ongoing basis but will need a financial accommodation only once or twice a year for an extremely large, out-of-the-norm billing which they simply cannot handle without some method of financing. Such periodic transactions are routinely accepted by roughly one half of all factors (see SPOT FACTORING). Business owners seeking a *spot factoring* arrangement must usually meet some rather strict guidelines and must also be prepared to pay substantially higher fees.

Factoring Styles

Factoring is one of the oldest known forms of commercial finance and though it has grown steadily through the centuries, its basic structure and list of services is still very similar to those found in transactions referenced during the Middle Ages. Over the centuries, factors have created many transactional programs to accommodate particular customer types. Today, factoring programs and specialty areas are expansive and nearly as numerous as the factors themselves. Still, the nuts and bolts basics of accounts receivable factoring remain the same and can actually be divided into just two major styles; *Maturity Factoring* and *Advance Factoring.*

Maturity Style Factoring

Maturity Factoring, with its historical roots imbedded firmly in the garment and textile industries, has been common in America since the 1920's and is known by a variety of other names such as *Traditional Factoring* or *Old Line Factoring.* All true maturity factoring arrangements are primarily structured around the factor's provision of credit and collection services rather than that of actually advancing cash for financing. In a standard maturity style factoring transaction:

FIRMLY IMBEDDED IN GARMENTS AND TEXTILES

- The factor provides credit analysis of a client's customer or group of customers.
- If not paid timely by the customer, the factor pays the owed amount upon credit approved accounts in an agreed upon number of days after sale, delivery, and invoicing.
- If a credit approved customer is unable to pay an invoice due to insolvency or bankruptcy, the factor provides payment as guarantor. There are no "advances" of cash made under a true maturity factoring arrangement. Payment is only made at the average maturity of the invoice batch if the purchased accounts remains unpaid.

NO ADVANCES OF CASH

As mentioned, maturity factoring is historically related to the garment and textile industries where it is still routinely found. In fact, some aspects of modern maturity factoring in America are easily traced back to the Colonial era of "king cotton". Because of the massive (and ever growing) amounts of offshore manufacturing now prevalent in this industry, true maturity factoring arrangements are no longer as common as they once were. In fact, recent polls of the industry reveal that well under twenty percent (20%) of all factors now offer a maturity-styled factoring product.

Advance Style Factoring (California Factoring)

CALIFORNIA FACTORING

Since maturity factors historically purchased and had control over a client's accounts receivable, a natural and eventual service addition to the maturity style was to provide some form of "pre-payment" or finance option upon the invoices purchased, rather than just traditional credit analysis and collection services. Such requests were already occurring on occasion in the maturity factoring arena and enough in fact, for some creative California-based factors to style a completely new type of factoring based upon an immediate advance of cash rather than just credit and collection services.

California factoring, most often called *advance factoring*, focused on industries other than garments and textiles and created a powerful new and accessible form of small business finance now available to cash-starved entrepreneurs nationwide. Unlike maturity factoring arrangements where the client expected to wait 30-60 days before payment was received, the new advance factors tended to put their clients on almost a C.O.D. basis. Advance factoring was initially directed towards smaller clients, typically those business owners generating under $150,000 in sales each month, since this was a business segment largely ignored by the nation's large maturity factors.

Once the advance factoring transaction was perfected, this new factoring style grew exponentially. Today, the advance style of factoring represents a strong majority of all transactions and an ever growing segment of the asset-based finance industry.

The Growth of Advance Factoring

NOTES

As the prevalence and popularity of the modern advance-style of factoring grew, hundreds of industry types and segments were added to the range of prospective factoring clients. It's now safe to say that the days of factoring services being primarily associated with the garment and textile industries have likely ended forever.

In a standard advance-styled factoring transaction today:

IMMEDIATE ADVANCE OF FUNDS ON PURCHASED ACCOUNTS

⇒ The factor advances funds on purchased accounts immediately with cash being wired directly into the client's business bank account.

⇒ The factor still provides expert credit analysis and collection service for the client's benefit.

⇒ If a credit approved customer is unable to pay an invoice due to insolvency or bankruptcy, the factor may make payment as the guarantor under *non-recourse* arrangements or may not under *recourse* arrangements. (See Recourse / Non-Recourse on the following page)

⇒ In a non-recourse arrangement, the factor's guaranty of payment only extends to matters of insolvency or bankruptcy of an approved customer and not trade disputes related to poor performance.

The Bottom Line

EXPLOSIVE GROWTH INTERNATIONALLY

Though California factoring originally tended to focus on small, entrepreneurial startups, that has changed over the years. Today, it is not unusual to find this method of factoring employed to finance businesses generating a $1,000,000 or even more in monthly receivables. Internationally, the growth of the advance style of factoring has been explosive and currently accounts for trillions of dollars of small business financing each and every year. Factoring brokers should be aware that maturity factoring still exists for the very rare occasion. Virtually all prospects you meet, however, will likely require the immediate provision of cash which is characteristic of the advance-styled transaction.

Recourse and Non-Recourse Factoring

One of the questions most often asked by prospective clients is: *What happens if one of my customers doesn't pay?* The answer depends on the kind of factoring facility provided or more accurately, whether the factoring arrangement is one of *recourse* or *non-recourse.*

FACTOR TAKES THE LOSS

As you already know, traditional factoring (maturity factoring) was a service which provided credit analysis and collections rather than financing. The factor paid the face value of invoices ONLY if the customer failed to pay within the allotted time under the terms of payment granted. Since the factor is the guarantor in a maturity factoring arrangement, all such arrangements are non-recourse by definition, meaning the factor has no option if the invoice is unpaid due to insolvency or bankruptcy. The factor takes the loss and pays the client.

Factoring brokers should strive to develop relationships with both recourse and non-recourse factors. In fact, many factors offer both services only with different cost structures. Some even offer a modified recourse product which has certain characteristics of both recourse and non-recourse factoring. When building your lenders database, make certain you create group segments for both recourse and non-recourse factors.

In modern advance factoring arrangements, factors can provide their services either on a *recourse* or on a *non-recourse* basis. Under a *non-recourse* method, the factor will be responsible for the losses on credit-accepted accounts which are not paid based on the insolvency or bankruptcy measure. Under a *recourse* method, however, the client is said to "warrant" the payment of the invoice by the customer. If the purchased invoice goes uncollected after a stipulated period of time (usually 90 days), the factor will charge back (force the repurchase of) the invoice to the client's account.

Its important to note that with the California-style of advance factoring, which generally tends to deal with smaller clients and often even smaller, marginal account debtor credits, non-recourse factoring simply doesn't provide the necessary service to the client who is primarily in need of financing and immediate cash under all circumstances.

Obviously, a factor is not going to agree to guarantee and purchase large amounts of invoices generated from sales to very small retailers that could realistically "close up shop" tomorrow.

So in some cases, small customers may be responsible for a relatively large portion of the total sales of the factor's client. In such instances where a client sells to a majority of small "mom and pop" businesses and establishments, the guarantees provided by non-recourse factoring are unrealistic and simply will not do the job. Only a recourse-style transaction can provide the much needed working capital and cash flow solutions.

Verification of Invoices

VERY HIGH QUALITY COLLATERAL

From a lender's viewpoint, accounts receivable are generally looked at as a very high-quality collateral. This is because invoices are self-liquidating. They will routinely be paid at or near their face value by the customer within a very short period of time and usually without so much as a collection call. And, even if there is a small deduction from full payment for a product flaw or poor service, such a deduction is seldom large enough to detrimentally effect the overall factoring transaction. The factor's advance is normally only at or near 80% of the invoice's face value, so the factor temporarily retains the balance as a "reserve" just for such occurrences.

FRAUD NOT UNCOMMON

Still, even though a very high-quality collateral, an invoice is a business asset very easily falsified. It is really only a piece of paper evidencing a commercial debt. Anyone can print thousands of fraudulent invoices from their home computer and submit them to a factor for purchase. Unfortunately, such attempts at fraud are not uncommon. This is why factors, with tens or even hundreds of thousands of dollars at risk on a single client advance, have become experts at the verification of invoices and the detection of fraud.

During the verification process, factors will contact a client's account debtors to ascertain the validity of invoices subject to advance. This is done prior to purchase and the factor's operations staff will most often verify an invoice by speaking directly with the purchasing or accounting department of a debtor. In cases where invoices involve physical goods and are of substantial size, factors may require a copy of a purchase order from the customer as well as shipping documents from the client to show that the order is valid and that the goods have actually been delivered. In some instances, the customer's accounts payable or receiving manager will be required to "sign off" on the invoice, evidencing the goods were received as ordered and that the invoice will be paid under normal terms of payment.

REQUIRED TO "SIGN OFF"

Fraud and the Independent Broker

Verification is always one of the most important steps in the factoring process but is of premier importance when it comes to a broker's new client submissions. Fortunately, verification has become quite a bit easier with the growth and expansion of the internet. It has, for example, become much easier to verify the true existence of account debtors and it is much more difficult to pass off a fake. Brokers should understand, however, that even though they are independent in the nature of their business relationship with a factor, they are also there to protect their financing source from fraud.

FIRST LINE OF DEFENSE AGAINST FRAUD

A well trained and knowledgeable independent broker is a factor's first line of defense against fraud. Factors will very often accept small factoring referrals without physically visiting the prospective client's business offices. For brokers, however, that is most often not the case. Most brokers work locally and will almost always call on their prospect at the workplace. And while factoring brokers never get involved in the actual contacting of account debtors and verification of an invoice, they should always stay alert and be tuned in to a prospect's local business operation, making certain it is legitimate, at least in its appearance. Always be alert for the possibility of fraud and a fraudulent client. If you sense anything wrong or not aboveboard when visiting a prospective client's office, report it to your factor immediately.

The Concept of Collateral

Factors, as you know, are members of the asset-based finance (ABF) community of lenders and as a group, all asset-based financiers operate based on the concept of *collateral.* What really sets this group apart from traditional "financial statement" lenders, such as most banks who gauge loan approval primarily on a borrower's financial strength, is that asset-based financiers focus more heavily on collateral assets and the ability to quickly liquidate a particular collateral in the event a financed party defaults on its obligations. For example, an equipment leasing company depends on its ability to repossess a piece of equipment and sell or re-lease it to recover or protect its invested capital if the lessee fails to make its timely lease payment.

COLLATERAL JUST A PLEDGE OF AN ASSET

Put simply, collateral is just a pledge of an asset which secures a borrower's repayment of a loan or similar financial accommodation. Anyone who has ever purchased a home is familiar with this concept with the mortgage lender having the right to *foreclose* on the real property if monthly payments are missed. The same is true for any business asset which is used to secure a commercial loan. In business finance, such lending is termed "secured lending", since the loan is secured or backed up by a collateral which can be liquidated in the event of default.

SECURED LENDING

For factors, collateral is the accounts receivable of their clients, even though true factoring is never a loan. As you know, factors actually purchase the accounts of a business at a discount and contractually, the business accounts (and rights to collection thereon) are *assigned* to the factor by the business owner at the time of purchase. The accounts are pledged as collateral for the factoring arrangement at the time of contracting. The factor then becomes sole owner of the accounts and when due, will receive payment directly from the seller's customer, the account debtor.

INCLUDES BOTH PURCHASED AND NON-PURCHASED ACCOUNTS

You should also know that in almost all instances, the pledge of accounts as collateral for a factoring facility includes both purchased and non-purchased invoices. In an event of default by the client, the factor has the right to collect on all invoices, purchased or not.

The Uniform Commercial Code

COLLATERAL FINANCED TWICE

Although the factor's purchase of the invoices through payment and assignment provides rights to collection, there exists another problem. What is to prevent a business owner from securing a loan from a bank or traditional lender, pledging its accounts to the bank as collateral, and then subsequently applying for a factoring arrangement and pledging the same accounts a second time to the factor? If done, the collateral would be financed twice and in theory, shared equally by both the factor and the bank. A battle surely would ensue to see who gets paid first in the event of default by the borrower. To prevent such a problem and enjoy a truly secure transaction, factors and lenders file a document called a *Uniform Commercial Code Financing Statement.*

ARTICLE 9

The *Uniform Commercial Code* (UCC) is a body of business related law that governs commercial transactions in all 50 states and especially those transactions involving the sale of goods, their transportation and delivery, and the payments upon such goods. The UCC is comprised of a series of *articles* or sections which, among their many focuses, define certain transactions and rights regarding those transactions. Included among these are sales, leases, deposit transactions, letters of credit, negotiable instruments, etc. Most important to factors and the asset-based finance community, is something called "Article 9", which deals with the laws and rules involving *secured transactions.*

When financing a company based on an asset or assets, a lender will file a "security interest" in the assets as collateral for the loan or financing. This filing document, called a *UCC-1 Financing Statement*, is said to "perfect" the lender's security interest in the collateral. In layman's terms, the UCC-1 filing:

- **notices the world that a financing is in place**
- **describes what specific collateral secures the loan**
- **determines the "pecking order" regarding who's entitled to the collateral in the event the borrower defaults on the loan.**

When filed, a UCC-1 is time stamped and in the world of UCCs, first to file wins. The first filer (lender) is said to be *senior* lender, and is entitled to collect upon the collateral first in the event of default. Second or lower position filers are *junior* lenders. In the event of default, a junior lender is only entitled to proceeds from the collateral after the senior lender is satisfied fully. In factoring financings, the factor must always be senior lender on accounts.

Searching the UCC for an Active Lien

SEARCHING THE UCC

When underwriting a new deal, one of the very first tasks a factor or any lender will perform is to search the appropriate UCC database to determine if the collateral for a loan is available or is already pledged and subject to lien by some previous lender or factor. The UCC requires that a UCC-1 security interest filing be:

⇒ **filed in the UCC filing database in the borrower's (client's) state of incorporation.**

⇒ **filed under the legal name of the borrower and exactly as it appears in the corporate records in the Secretary of State's office.**

Such a standardized filing and database system makes determining the availability of any collateral a relatively simple process. Lenders can search confidently for current active UCC filings on most business collaterals.

As you know, factors must have a senior 1st position lien on accounts in order to provide financing. If a search of the UCC filing database evidences a current active filing upon a prospective client where the client's accounts receivable are pledged, the ability to finance the prospect through factoring is prohibited unless:

⇒ **the current lender will *subordinate* (release) its senior position on accounts. (This will normally only occur if the lender has an abundance of other assets it can use to collateralize the loan).**

SUBORDINATE ITS LIEN POSITION

⇒ **the existing loan is of such a small size that the factor's initial cash advance upon invoices can pay off the loan's balance and *take out* the previous lender.**

Even prior to the final contracts with a client being signed, it is not unusual for the factor to file a UCC-1 financing statement to secure its first lien position in accounts. In some instances of fraud, a borrower will apply to multiple lenders at the same time, attempting to quickly secure financing more than once on the same asset and thus defrauding the lender.

UCC-3 AMENDMENT STATEMENT

In the event the contracting with the new client is not finalized and does not occur, the factor will simply release its lien. Such a lien release is performed by filing a UCC-3 amendment statement which is used to extend, modify or to terminate an existing UCC-1 financing statement.

Notification of Assignment

Once invoices are purchased, factors monitor their investment and turn to collections. In fact, at this point factors are simply "waiters", but not the kind you might find in your favorite restaurant. Factors wait for THEIR money on THEIR invoices. The use of "their" is emphasized here because as you know, factoring is a purchase and sale transaction and never a loan. Factors own the invoices.

Once purchased, the invoice is assigned and the factor is the legal owner of the invoice and has all rights to the invoice payment. In fact, if a factor's client receives a payment on an assigned invoice and doesn't immediately remit that payment to the factor, it can be construed as civil theft with varying legal ramifications and penalties, depending on the state of jurisdiction. In the industry this is called a *misdirected payment* or more commonly, *collection.*

To help avoid such problems of misdirected payments, factors will notify a client's customers of the invoice purchase, assignment of rights, and the existing financing arrangement in a process called *notification of assignment.* The rules regarding such notification are set forth in Article 9 of the UCC and basically state that once legally noticed, the account debtor's payment obligation is now to the noticer (factor or lender) and no longer to the borrower (client).

All Invoices of the Account Debtor

When a client's customer receives notification, the notification pertains to ALL invoices currently payable or payable in the future. It includes invoices factored as well as those invoices not factored. UCC law is written to be very black and white with little gray area for lawyers to argue over. Although the client may have an arrangement with a factor under which all invoices of a customer do not have to be factored 100% of the time, all invoice payments must, none the less, be made to the factor's address whether they were financed or not. Payments made to the factor on invoices not purchased will simply "flow through" to the client's bank account when reserve distributions are made.

NON-FACTORED PAYMENTS FLOW THROUGH

If properly (legally) noticed, the account debtor has really no option but to pay the factor going forward. To ignore the factor's notification of assignment is to risk being sued and forced to make payment on an invoice a second time. Requiring ALL invoice payments of a noticed customer to be made to the factor preserves the legal integrity of the notification and there will be little available defense for the account debtor based on confusion or ambiguity if legal action is ever necessary.

In many states, basic UCC searches are free and brokers will be able to access the service. If available to you at no cost, always do a UCC search on any prospective client prior to submitting a deal to a factor.

Learning to use the UCC properly can be an excellent method of prospecting. You will, for example, be able to explore active businesses financings in the state, determine if it's the type of business that can also benefit from factoring, and create a marketing campaign based on that probability. Don't, however, use a UCC search in an attempt to "steal" business from a lender.

LEARN TO USE THE UCC PROPERLY

Factoring Advance Rates

When contracting with a new client, the factor will determine an *initial advance rate* (percentage rate) upon invoices it purchases. Throughout the industry, the most common rate of advance is 80%, but on occasion, factors will advance 85%, 90%, or even higher. This higher advance rate can occur in situations where the account debtors are exceptionally strong, creditworthy payers and the payment for goods sold or service performed has very little chance of being reduced with credit memos, spoilage, chargebacks, etc.

HOLDBACK KNOWN AS RETAINAGE

Initial advance percentage rates can also vary markedly depending on the client's industry. For example in the construction industry, where a 10% payment holdback is common (this is known in the construction industry as *retainage*), the advance rates on purchased invoices might be 70% instead of the more common 80%. This is to protect the factor from shortfalls caused by the 10% retainage holdback.

Advance rates on invoiced sales where the invoice amounts are very small may also be subject to slightly lower advance rates simply due to the overall increase in expense to the factor in processing such small transactions. Contrarily, clients who present large invoices for purchase with very strong, creditworthy customers are often provided with both higher advance rates and lower factoring fees.

NOTE: When explaining the advance to prospective clients, its important for them to know the advance is just the initial payment and there is more to come after the customer's payment is received. Do not let the prospect think that the factor is purchasing the invoices for 80% and that's all they will get. Make sure they know there will be an additional rebate after payment is received.

The Factor's Reserve

The percentage of the face value of the invoice not initially advanced is referred to as the *factor's reserve.* An initial advance rate of 80%, for example, means the client will receive a wire of cash for 80% of the invoice face value. The 20% balance not advanced remains on the books as *reserve* or more specifically, *uncollected reserve.*

80% INITIAL ADVANCE
20% RESERVE

Uncollected reserve is simply a bookkeeping entry and represents an anticipated amount of additional cash to be available when the purchased invoice is paid. Once a payment is actually received, *uncollected reserve,* the bookkeeping entry, becomes *cash reserve* and such additional cash, less the factor's service fee, is then available to be paid to the client through what is termed a *reserve distribution,* or more often referred to as a *rebate.*

The availability for reserve rebates or distributions actually depends on certain circumstances. For example, does the client have some additional invoices which are aged over 90 days and in jeopardy of being charged back or are there invoices not being paid due to a trade dispute? Are there unforeseen expenses such as legal or tax expenses which must be paid by the factor for the client's benefit? If so, cash reserve generated from one invoice or a group of invoices may be temporarily held to guarantee the factor's repayment for the advance on the disputed invoice or to pay certain required expenses.

AVAILABILITY AFFECTED BY CHARGE-BACKS

The amount of uncollected reserve scheduled for rebate will also be reduced by the earned *factoring fees* before it can distributed. Once a payment is received from a customer, that check payment and detail information will be entered into the factor's invoice tracking software and credited to the appropriate invoice. Factoring fees will be tallied and deducted, a collection report will be generated, and if there are no other circumstances which would prevent it, a reserve distribution (rebate) is then ready to be made to the client.

Factoring Fee Structures

When you begin to market the factoring product to small business owners, you will naturally be asked questions regarding how factoring works, how it will solve a particular problem, how fast can it be put in place, etc. One of the most common questions regarding factoring will naturally be: *How much does it cost?*

MASTER PURCHASE AND SALES AGREEMENT

The methods by which fees are charged by a factor are set forth in their factoring contracts (often called *Master Purchase and Sales Agreements*) and although there are hundreds of derivations, fee structures generally fall into just one of two basic categories:

- **FEES CHARGED IN WINDOWS**
- **FLAT-FEE PLUS INTEREST FEES**

Fees Charged in Windows

Fee structures using this method are very common among small and mid-size factors with the most common windows being 10 or 15 days. A sample of this fee structure can be seen below for a $100,000 invoice, advanced at an 80% rate, and a fee of 1% for each window (roughly two-percent per month). Window fees are usually charged on the face amount of the invoice, not the advance amount.

DAY	FEE	REBATE	TOTAL PAID
1-15	$1,000	$19,000	$99,000
16-30	$2,000	$18,000	$98,000
31-45	$3,000	$17,000	$97,000
46-60	$4,000	$16,000	$96,000
61-75	$5,000	$15,000	$95,000
76-90	$6,000	$14,000	$94,000

Using the previous "windows" table, you can calculate that an invoice of $100,000 outstanding for 40 days would be charged a factoring fee of $3,000 (31-45 day rate) or 3% of the invoice face value. Once the invoice is paid in full, the factor will repay itself the advanced amount of $80,000 leaving $20,000 additional funds due to the client as a rebate. Prior to wiring those funds to the client, however, the factor will reduce that amount by deducting the factoring fee earned amount of $3,000, thus leaving a net rebate of $17,000.

Flat-Fee Plus Interest Fee Rates

Fee structures using this method are very common among larger factors wanting to make their fees more resemble those of asset-based lending. Here, a fixed discount is charged on the invoice face amount for the factoring services of credit analysis, collections, and operations. An interest component is also charged on the cash amount advanced. That is added to the fixed discount for a total financing fee.

BASE RATE PLUS MARGIN

The interest component is usually pegged to the published prime rate, LIBOR (London Interbank Offered Rate) rate or the 10 year U.S. Treasury Rate which acts as a *base rate* of interest. A *margin* for profit is then added to the base rate of interest which represents the total interest component charged. An example can be seen below for a $100,000 invoice, advanced at 80%, with a flat factoring discount of 3% and 12% fixed simple interest rate for each 10 day period.

DAY	DISCOUNT	INTEREST	REBATE	TOTAL
10	$3,000	$263	$16,732	$96,732
20	$3,000	$526	$16,474	$96,474
30	$3,000	$789	$16,211	$96,211
40	$3,000	$1,052	$15,948	$95,948
50	$3,000	$1,315	$15,685	$95,685
60	$3,000	$1,578	$15,422	$95,422
70	$3,000	$1,841	$15,159	$95,159
80	$3,000	$2,104	$14,896	$94,896
90	$3,000	$2,367	$14,633	$94,633

Using the example chart of a flat-fee plus interest method, you can see that a client's $100,000 invoice advanced at an 80% rate ($80,000) and outstanding for 60 days would have been charged a 3% flat factoring fee or $3,000 and would have accrued an interest charge of $1,578 for a total finance fee of $4,578.

NO REAL COMPETITIVE ADVANCE

Generally speaking, those factors using a window style structure will have slightly lower fees for invoices paid in less than 30 days. Flat-fee plus interest factors will be slightly less expensive for clients with invoices paid in more than 30 days. In the real world, with the broad diversity of fee structures, hybrids, and combinations found throughout the industry, a factoring fee structure needs to be examined closely to determine if one has a competitive advantage over another for a particular client. Additionally, most factors are reasonably flexible with their fee structures and accommodative modifications necessary to suit a particular fee-sensitive client are very common.

The Bottom Line

When you begin to market factoring to small business owners and even referral sources, the subject of fees will always come up. Incredibly, too many CPA-types will look at a factoring fee of 2 1/2 percent for 30 days and say something like: *That's 30% per year. I could never recommend that to my clients unless they were desperate.* That calculation is, of course, ridiculous. The truth is, if a business provides 30 day terms of payment to its customers, the costs of factoring are about the same as taking a credit card. In fact, in some cases, its cheaper.

FEE RATES ABOUT THE SAME AS CREDIT CARDS

Credit card industry statistics show the average finance cost for a not-in-store credit card swipe to be 2.30% - 2.50%. The 30 day factoring fee for an average size client is about the same at 2.50%. Just like a credit card sale, factoring is a "transactional" method of finance. You cannot multiply the 30 day rate by 12 to get an annual fee rate because the fees stop as soon as the invoice is paid. They do not go on for a year. When you add in the additional services of the factor such as expert credit analysis and collections, you can build a strong case that factoring is a bargain when compared to accepting credit cards.

Invoice Tracking Software

When a client's account is approved and invoices purchased, there's a lot of information which needs to be monitored and tracked. Documents must be prepared, reports generated (including your monthly commission report), and collection notes stored. All of this is the job of the factor's *invoice tracking software.* Among its many tasks, invoice tracking software:

- **Generates Advance Schedules and Collection Reports**
- **Generates Client Aging Reports and Monthly Statements**
- **Keeps Records of Notification and Verification**
- **Calculates Factoring Fees and Interest Charges**
- **Keeps Collection Records and Notes**
- **Monitors Credit Exposure and Concentrations**
- **Accounts for Checks and Wire Transfers**
- **Generates Client Year End Tax Statements**
- **Most Importantly...Generates Commission Reports**

GENERATES BROKER COMMISSION REPORTS

The Collections Process

All factors will become involved in the collection and payment process upon purchased invoices and will typically have in-house personnel assigned to that task. Each month, factors will generate monthly statements of account which will be mailed to all account debtors of all clients. The statements of account will list all invoices outstanding and will be directed to the customer's accounts payable department. Courteous collection calls will be made to check up on those payments which have not been received by their due date.

Some new factoring clients may be concerned about the factor's staff contacting their clients and being too harsh in collections. In reality, there is really no need to worry here. A factor's collectors are highly trained professionals who are well aware of the relationship between client and customer. They are also aware that mistreating customers can lead to a client leaving a particular factor to seek another.

Factoring in History

As a factoring broker, the better you understand your product, the higher the value of your "personal stock". As we have already discussed, consultants have value because they are experts in their particular field. It is easily understood that the more you know about factoring, the more you will be looked at as an expert and likely beneficiary of referral business sent your way from other local professionals.

Unknown to most, factoring has a rich and colorful history and learning about its contributions to business finance throughout the ages can be important when it comes to networking and a good idea for any serious factoring broker.

An Ancient Source of Business Finance

Factoring is often referenced as having its roots traced as far back as the 18th century BC and the ancient Babylonians, although you can probably say this about all types of commercial finance. At that time, the city-state of Babylon was ruled by the much celebrated Amorite king, *Hammurabi*, drafter of the *Laws of Hammurabi*. Among its 282 decrees, these laws set forth various guidelines for merchant transactions of the day and rules for the repayment of certain types of business debts.

True factoring-styled transactions become more recognizable at later points in history and particularly throughout the Mediterranean trade corridors. Phoenicians, the greatest traders of their day, are said to have employed factoring-related finance transactions as they ventured to foreign ports.

Characteristically, factoring services throughout the ages usually involved the service of *warehousing* goods and not just that of financing. This important additional feature, unknown today, did not really fade away until the early 19th century.

Ancient traders depended heavily on trustworthy warehousing agents for their export goods who would:

- ⇒ **take physical possession of goods on consignment**
- ⇒ **warehouse the goods**
- ⇒ **act as sales agents and find buyers for the goods**
- ⇒ **collect payment upon sales for the selling trader**

PROMISSORY NOTES AT A DISCOUNT

In ancient Rome, it was common for producers to employ the services of a "mercantile agent" to manage the sale of and assure delivery and payment for goods. There is also evidence that the Romans formalized methods and regulations for the sale of promissory notes at a discount, a direct characteristic related to modern factoring.

The Roots of Modern Factoring

BLACKWELL HALL FACTORS

The roots of what can be called "modern factoring" are traced to the textile trade in England during the 17th century and *Blackwell Hall. Blackwell Hall*, originally built in 1397, acted as a merchant clearing house for the cloth trade, England's primary commodity of that era. *Blackwell Hall Factors* acted as fee-based group of agents who monopolized the handling of the sale of textiles.

By the end of the 17th century, there were roughly fifty factors at *Blackwell Hall* who sold the raw materials to manufacturers and then additionally provided credit to clothiers, drapers, and the various exporters of the day. Throughout this period of English colonization, English factors were used to facilitate trade between Britain and her colonies, and especially her highly-prized American Colonies.

Factoring Arrives in America

NAVIGATION ACTS

During America's Colonial Era, factors provided payment advances to the colonists for shipments of cotton, furs, tobacco, and timber. As set forth in regulations contained in the *Navigation Acts* of the day, the colonists were strictly forbidden to manufacture goods in direct competition with the "mother country". They had little choice but to send raw materials to England, but to do so, required the services of a trustworthy "middleman" who could be counted on to transact the business. The middleman was, of course, the period's trade factors and the services provided by such factors survived America's War of Independence, with little change in methods for many decades to follow.

FACTORS WALK

During the 19th century and the heyday of "king cotton", industry cotton factors provided substantial funding for exports to Europe which accounted for nearly 80% of America's annual cotton crop. The historic warehouse district known as *Factors Walk,* in Savannah, Georgia, still evidences the importance of factoring during this period and in the history of this vital commodity.

MERCANTILE CREDIT CORPORATION

The actual birth of modern factoring in America is most associated with the creation of the *Mercantile Credit Corporation* which was established in 1904. It is considered to be the first true commercial finance company. *Mercantile* was started by two encyclopedia salesmen, Arthur Jones and John Little, who were well acquainted with the need for creating time payments related to their book sales. They wondered if such *installment financing* based on accounts receivable as collateral might be suitable for other industries. The factors had been using similar financing methods for centuries although almost exclusively in the textile industry.

After some initial successes and the creation of *Mercantile,* competition quickly entered the market with the formation of St. Louis-based industry giant *Commercial Credit & Investment Company* (CIT) and also Baltimore-based *Commercial Credit Company,* both being started around the same time. All of these early institutional lenders initially focused on developing installment payment systems for asset finance rather than the more expansive credit and collection services provided by the factors.

As an important feature, these early asset-based finance companies structured and provided services without notification to account debtors. Notification was a perceived stigma of factoring which discredited users and evidenced a level of financial weakness.

INSTALLMENT PAYMENT PROGRAMS

It did not take long for these early lenders to begin offering types of installment payment programs for automobiles, appliances, and many other consumer "pleasure" purchases of the time. The installment finance industry began to expand exponentially with lenders eventually offering unsecured financing products in addition to those styled as asset-based loans.

As for factoring, it still flourished in the garment and textile industries since it provided the much needed services of credit and collections characteristically required with the period's large retailers. From the banking and asset-based lending viewpoint, factoring was still looked upon as a financial accommodation for weak, undercapitalized manufacturers and suppliers selling goods to retail companies considered to be "sub-prime" credits.

Postwar America saw a significant transition in the factoring industry as large banks and asset-based lenders realized there was additional business to be had by embracing this popular method of financing. Although factoring had still not shed its image as a financing method of last resort for businesses of marginal credit, the banks came to realize that since they were providing the investment capital to finance the nation's factors, they were really exposing themselves to the same sub-prime lending risks by proxy. So the large banks made the decision to begin purchasing and acquiring the nation's leading textile factors.

LOWER RATES AND NEW LEGITIMACY

A positive result of the entry of the competitive banks into the factoring industry was lower financing rates. Well established banking names also added a new legitimacy to the industry and in general, factoring began the process of building respect as a primary source of business finance. Also during this consolidation period, factoring began to expand its service areas to include not just garments and textiles, but hundreds of other industries and product areas. Factoring grew rapidly through the 1970s and 80s resulting in the creation of factoring giants such as *CIT*, *GMAC*, *HSBC*, *Heller*, *Rosenthal & Rosenthal*, *Milberg*, and many others.

TAKE THE QUIZ

Chapter 2 Quiz

1. Factoring is considered a method of ________
   A. asset-based finance
   B. real estate finance
   C. floorplan finance
   D. none of the above

2. In factoring terminology, an invoice is also known as ________________
   A. purchase order
   B. a bill of lading
   C. a purchase contract
   D. an account

3. A business selling invoices to a factor is a ______________
   A. customer
   B. client
   C. borrower
   D. both A & C

4. Factors always purchase accounts receivable ____________
   A. at full face value
   B. at a discount
   C. at a premium
   D. all of the above

5. The business obligated to pay on a purchased invoice is the ________________
   A. customer
   B. account debtor
   C. client
   D. both A & B above

6. In a non-recourse factoring arrangement, the factor absorbs the loss of account debtor non-payment in the event of _______
   A. bankruptcy
   B. insolvency
   C. trade disputes
   D. Both A & B above

7. An initial disbursement of funds upon purchased invoices is known as _________________

   A. a rebate
   B. a reserve distribution
   C. an advance
   D. a initial charge-back

TAKE THE QUIZ

8. Factoring is _________________

   A. never a loan
   B. always between two parties
   C. similar to leasing
   D. both B & C above

9. Factoring is ___________________

   A. a purchase and sale transaction
   B. always between three parties
   C. a discount financing mechanism
   D. all of the above

10. Factoring finances __________________

   A. invoices
   B. accounts
   C. B2B sales
   D All of the above

11. Invoices tendered to a factor for purchase which represents goods not yet delivered are considered _________________

   A. consignment invoices
   B. contras
   C subject invoices
   D. pre-ship invoices

12 A condition where a client and its customer both sell to each other with the risk of offsetting amounts due is called a contra.

   A. True
   B. False

ANSWERS TO THESE AND OTHER QUESTIONS CAN BE FOUND IN THE BACK OF THE GUIDE

NICHES & ESSENTIAL PRODUCT AREAS

Expanding Your Horizons

NOTES

CORE PRODUCT AREAS

Now that you understand the transactional basics of factoring, its time to learn a little about the many specialty *niche* areas of this unique form of commercial finance and also about four additional and important "core" product areas for brokers.

The majority of factors are what might be called "plain vanilla". They will look favorably at most standard factoring deals which do not involve problems of mechanics liens, spoilage, or additional special paperwork that can elevate non-payment risk. They keep it as simple as possible and avoid industries and sectors they are not completely comfortable with.

SPECIALTY TRANSACTIONS

The occasional need to finance hard to fund, non-standard factoring transactions, however, will often attract a small group of very creative, entrepreneurial factors who learn to deal with the additional transactional risks and adversities present. In fact, such specialty factors may actually adjust their business models and marketing efforts towards that particular difficult industry or segment. These "niche" factors play an important industry role and brokers should become knowledgeable regarding their capabilities.

So among the many industry areas brokers should understand inside and out is the area of niche factoring, or how factors deal with the unusual or exceptional risks associated with a particular industry. If contacted by a small business owner operating in such an industry and seeking your expertise, you will obviously need to have that knowledge at the ready and in your ammo belt.

SPECIALIZING IN CONSTRUCTION RECEIVABLES

Another reason to expand your horizons and explore factoring's many specialized areas is that some will offer brokers a significant marketing and operational advantage. In fact, gaining this special knowledge and focusing on a particular industry segment can provide you with a tremendous advantage over your competition. Specializing in construction receivables factoring, for example, can often provide well prepared brokers with such a powerful opportunity that it is literally the only sector where they need focus their marketing efforts.

In the balance of this chapter, you will be introduced to the most common areas referred to as "niche areas" by factors. Rest assured, there are probably more being created as you read this guide. In each niche area, we will also provide you with the reasons for the difficulty in financing such industries or transactions. Getting to know the following specialized and hard to finance industries will be very helpful to you when you begin marketing your business.

NICHE AREAS OF FACTORING

- CONSTRUCTION RECEIVABLES
- STAFFING & TEMP SERVICES
- AGRICULTURAL RECEIVABLES
- FEDERAL / STATE GOVERNMENT RECEIVABLES
- REAL ESTATE COMMISSIONS
- FREIGHT BILL / TRUCKING
- THIRD PARTY MEDICAL RECEIVABLES
- DIP (DEBTOR-IN-POSSESSION) FINANCING
- SPOT FACTORING
- MICRO-FACTORING
- POULTRY AND MEAT PROCESSING RECEIVABLES
- INTERNATIONAL (CROSS-BORDER)

In addition to these specialized niche areas of factoring, we will also introduce you to four "must know" essential CORE product areas for all factoring brokers. These are:

ADDITIONALCORE PRODUCT AREAS

- **ASSET-BASED LENDING**
- **PURCHASE ORDER FINANCE**
- **MERCHANT CASH ADVANCE**
- **MICROLOANS**

As we previously mentioned, you may occasionally hear references to certain types of consumer financing transactions referred to as factoring. For example, the financing of true legal receivables, invoices payable by businesses to law firms for services rendered, is a commonly factored transaction. There are other specialized finance companies, however, that provide cash advances to plaintiff parties (individuals) involved in personal injury lawsuit claims. Such advances are strictly based on the merits of the case and the likelihood of an award being granted. These *pre-settlement legal advances* are often referred to as factoring transactions, yet they do not involve an invoice nor or they typically B2B in nature.

PRE-SETTLEMENT LEGAL ADVANCES

Finance companies specializing in the purchase of the monthly income streams provided by *structured settlements* and annuities are said to "factor" those income streams. Here again, no invoice is involved and the advance is made to an individual and not a business. Even a future inheritance that is tied up in the probate court system can be factored or advanced upon at a discount (called an *inheritance advance*).

STRUCTURED SETTLEMENTS

INHERITANCE ADVANCES

Well informed freelance brokers should probably be aware of such quasi-factoring products, even if they tend to stretch the boundaries of what is considered to be "true" factoring. They are a type of financing based on discounting, just like factoring, and whose providers are well known to pay attractive fees and commissions for referrals. Such consumer-based, specialized areas of finance are much smaller than the factoring and asset-based finance industries, but doing a little online research and including these products in your knowledge base may well provide you with an occasional opportunity to earn additional fee and commission income.

Additional Essential Product Areas

There are many types of business finance included under the heading of *Asset-Based Finance.* You have already been introduced to a very powerful type, that of accounts receivable factoring. There are many others used to finance small and mid-size businesses worldwide. Some, such as *equipment leasing*, you have probably heard of or may have even utilized. Others, such as *forfaiting*, a rather exotic method of financing large, cross-border sales in emerging markets, is unknown to all but a few industry experts.

FORFAITING & CROSS BORDER SALES

Before getting totally immersed in factoring's many nook and cranny niche areas, we're going to introduce you to four important and essential CORE products you need to learn about before you ever open your doors as a broker. They are *asset-based lending, purchase order finance, merchant cash advances*, and *micro-lending.* Along with factoring, they make up the primary product areas all factoring brokers must have in their playbook to begin operation. For most freelance consultants, these five areas will account for virtually 100% of the commissions and fees earned year after year.

Asset-Based Lending

Asset-Based Lending is a well-practiced method of business finance and ready source of working capital which is typically used to:

⇒ **accelerate cash flow on accounts receivable**

⇒ **finance the manufacturing of goods for purchase orders**

⇒ **finance business inventory**

⇒ **acquire business assets**

⇒ **manage turnarounds**

Asset based loans are simply working capital loans secured by lien rights to a collateral, but should be distinguished from more traditional bank loans or what can be termed *financial statement loans.* Here's the difference:

- ***Financial Statement Loans:*** are loans which are based on the financial strength, creditworthiness, and balance sheet health of the borrower. They reflect on the borrower's calculated ability to repay the loan from normal operations and cash flow and are often the most difficult types of loans to obtain for young companies.
- ***Asset-Based Loans:*** are loans primarily based on the liquidation value of business assets. Such assets will include accounts receivable, inventory, and occasionally equipment. They are perceived as higher risk loans than financial statement loans but are easier to obtain for younger companies with a limited credit history.

HIGHER RISK FINANCING

So the real difference between asset-based lending and traditional commercial bank lending is simply how the lender views its primary source of security and repayment for the loan. The security for a traditional loan is cash flow and a strong balance sheet. The security for an asset-based loan is accounts receivable, inventory, equipment, and the fair market liquidation value of those assets.

FAIR MARKET LIQUIDATION VALUE

ABL Revolving Line of Credit

The actual loan structure of a typical asset-based loan also differs significantly from a financial statement loan. A financial statement loan will most often be structured as a *term loan* or *amortized fixed loan* with the loan amount being determined and fixed at the loan's time of creation. Although they often are used to address problems of cash flow, they can be used for almost any purpose including equipment purchases or acquisitions.

An asset-based loan will usually be structured as a *revolving line of credit* with a primary focus of addressing problems of cash flow. The line of credit available to the business owner will have a maximum cap, but will also expand and contract based on the amount of current business accounts receivable outstanding and the amount of inventory on hand.

REVOLVING LINE OF CREDIT

Asset-Based Loan Collateral

Asset-based loan collateral will normally include the accounts receivable, inventory, and perhaps the equipment of a business. If a business also owns real estate, it is usually financed in a separate long-term amortized transaction and not considered part of the asset-based loan's collateral.

THE INITIAL BORROWING BASE

The maximum amount of an asset based loan will be determined by a formula. The results of the loan formula will determine the loan's *initial borrowing base.* A typical asset-based loan formula might be calculated on:

⇒ **ACCOUNTS RECEIVABLE:** 80% of the face value of eligible accounts receivable (just like factoring)

⇒ **INVENTORY:** 50% - 70% of the estimated liquidation value of inventory

⇒ **EQUIPMENT:** 50% - 70% of the liquidation value of the equipment

A/R Assignment & Collection Schedules

To help determine the available credit line, an asset-based borrower will prepare two schedules each week and forward them to the asset-based lender. These are the:

⇒ **ACCOUNTS ASSIGNMENT SCHEDULE:** lists all new accounts receivable billings for the week in numerical order. New accounts considered eligible will increase the borrowing base.

⇒ **ACCOUNTS COLLECTION SCHEDULE:** documents all collections upon outstanding accounts and will reduce the borrowing base.

Based on these two reports, the asset-based lender will prepare a *Borrowing Base Certificate* which calculates the new maximum amount of credit available to the borrower under the revolving line.

Asset-based lending is most often structured on a non-notification basis or in other words, customers of the borrower are unaware of the financing. Payments received each week, however, are either directly remitted to or forwarded to a special depository account known as the *cash collateral account* which is often a lockbox at a local bank. Cash deposits made to this account act to reduce the loan balance in the revolving line. They also reduce the interest being charged and increase the borrowing base.

CASH COLLATERAL ACCOUNT

Verification of Invoices

As in factoring, asset-based lenders will periodically verify invoices and their amounts to detect if fraud is present. This can be done by mailing monthly statements of account to the borrower's customers or through direct customer contact. The primary function of the verification process is to detect fraudulent invoices which may have been submitted to artificially increase the borrowing base. Such periodic verifications usually involve just a sampling of the borrower's customers, but if fraud is suspected or detected, will involve all.

PROCESS TO DETECT FRAUD

Field Examinations

Another characteristic of asset-based lending is periodic on-site field examinations which will:

⇒ **validate the borrower's reporting and accounting**

⇒ **substantiate the value and condition of collateral including inventory**

⇒ **disclose issues which may materially affect the loan's overall condition**

⇒ **detect a deteriorating situation**

Such field examinations are a necessity and tend to be more frequent in large loans with a substantial inventory component. While borrower fraud involving accounts receivable is relatively easy to detect, inventory is another matter. In desperate times, inventory has a nasty habit of "growing legs" and walking out the door.

Purchase Order Finance

Purchase order finance is an ancillary product and financing tool provided by many factors as well as stand alone providers. It is an important form of finance too often associated only with import-export trade, although it is perfectly suited for domestic transactions as well.

When submitting their first deals, many new brokers are not aware of the difference between factoring (invoice finance), purchase order finance, and contract finance. All brokers need to learn that...

- **FACTORING:** is the purchase of invoices where the goods or services represented on the invoice have already been delivered or services performed.
- **PURCHASE ORDER FINANCE:** is a method of financing the actual manufacture of goods so they may be delivered in accordance to a valid purchase order. Purchase order finance is readily available to most businesses involved in offshore contract manufacturing where a large order for goods is received from a quality creditworthy customer.
- **CONTRACT FINANCE:** Not to be confused with contract manufacturing, this refers to the financing of a contract (typically service related) where some form of *mobilization funds* are needed to begin the performance of services as set forth in the contract.

THE BIGGEST MISTAKE MADE BY NEW INDUSTRY BROKERS

THE BIGGEST MISTAKE MADE BY NEW INDUSTRY BROKERS

Without question, the biggest mistake made by new brokers is referring clients to a factor who have just been awarded a service contract and are seeking mobilization funds. This is contract finance. The work has not been performed, and no invoice is involved. It is not factoring nor is it purchase order finance. There is no collateral and it will always be turned down.

Purchase order finance commonly involves the need for financing the manufacture of goods when a large order is received which is in excess of the amount of inventory on hand and/or the available capital to make the goods.

Basically, a purchase order is a contract that guarantees payment for goods delivered if the goods arrive to specification and by a particular date. Purchase order finance is a method of financing the production of those goods so the order can be met. Once the order is shipped and delivered, it can then be invoiced and if required, that invoice can be factored. The criteria necessary for purchase order finance is as follows:

FINANCES THE PRODUCTION OF GOODS

- ⇒ **A Valid Order:** There must be a valid order from a creditworthy customer. The ability of the customer to pay for the goods once delivered is critical in a purchase order transaction.
- ⇒ **Performance Capability:** The client must have a track record and performance history showing its ability to make the goods (or have the goods made through contract manufacturing) and meet specifications and deadlines as set forth in the purchase order.
- ⇒ **Inability to Modify:** The purchase order must be "firm" in that its price and quantities cannot be adjusted or modified. Additionally, the order must warrant that if the goods are delivered according to specification and deadline, they will be paid for unconditionally.

CRITERIA REQUIRED

In most instances, a purchase order finance company will post a *letter of credit* (in an amount necessary to manufacture the goods) with a bank acceptable to the manufacturer. Once the goods are made to specification, samples accepted by the customer, and the order shipped, the letter of credit is "triggered" and the product manufacturer is paid. The goods are then delivered directly to the customer. The customer will be billed for the delivered goods and the invoice factored if necessary to "take out" the purchase order finance company. In some cases, the purchase order finance company and the factor are one in the same and the two separate financings are seamlessly blended.

LETTER OF CREDIT IS POSTED

Double Broker Commissions

DOUBLE COMMISSIONS

For industry brokers, purchase order finance usually provides an opportunity to earn "double commissions". This is because the vast majority of purchase order financings require the purchase order finance company to be paid off (taken out) as soon as the goods are shipped to or received by the customer.

Purchase order finance usually involves large, out-of-the norm orders and most often, the client utilizing purchase order finance does not have the ready cash to pay the purchase order finance company off when the goods are delivered. Most will not have the funds until the customer actually pays the invoice for the shipment. A factor, is therefor, required to advance against the invoice and subsequently pay off the purchase order finance company using a portion of the funds from the initial advance.

PACIFIC RIM MANUFACTURERS

It is very common to find the need for purchase order funding in the small manufacturing sector and especially when a domestic manufacturer is actually contract manufacturing with a factory located in the Pacific Rim. Such offshore production facilities will almost always require the posting of a letter of credit to produce the goods. Letters of credit are complex trade documents best drawn up by experts such as purchase finance companies.

LIFE-OF-ACCOUNT COMMISSIONS

When selecting a funding source for any deal involving purchase order finance and factoring, search your lender database for a factor that provides both rather than two separate entities. This will insure that you become the broker of record for both transactions. Additionally, make certain the financing source for the purchase order finance pays life-of-account commissions for referrals. While almost all do, there are a select few that only pay the purchase order referral fee for the first year.

Referral commissions paid to brokers for purchase order finance are very similar to factoring with the referring broker usually earning 15% or more of the fees earned. In almost all purchase order funding transactions, the referring broker will earn both a percentage of the purchase order finance fees as well as a percentage of the factoring fees.

Merchant Cash Advance

Like several other financing types presented in this section, MCAs or *Merchant Cash Advances* and their related *ACH Advances* are not true factoring transactions. Their popularity with seasoned factoring brokers and their small business clients is such that you need to become familiar with this particular product segment of the asset-based finance industry.

SHORT TERM LUMP SUM ADVANCE

Originally, MCAs were structured as a short term lump sum advance to a business in return for an agreed upon percentage of the business's future credit card receipts. The MCA provider would partner with the credit card service provider of a business to effect a daily or weekly withdrawal for repayment of the advance. In some cases, the MCA provider would require that it actually become the credit card processor. Advance repayments were setup to be of short term duration, usually 18 months or less.

PURCHASE AND SALE TRANSACTIONS

Much like factoring, MCAs are not loans but purchase and sale discount transactions, thus allowing the MCA to charge higher than normal fee rates and not be in violation of state *usury laws*. In a typical MCA transaction, a business owner might sell $20,000 of its future credit card sales for a discounted price of $15,000 in immediate cash. The entire $20,000 is then collected over an 8 to 10 month period.

NO PERSONAL GUARANTEES

The term merchant cash advance has now grown to include a host of small business financing alternatives, many of which are not directly associated with credit cards, but simply daily sales deposits. Although overall costs of MCAs are considered high, there is also considerable risk to the MCA provider in such transactions. Since MCAs are not loans, there are usually no personal guarantees required from a business owner in such financings. If the business receiving the MCA cash advance becomes insolvent prior to repaying the advance, the MCA provider must absorb the loss.

The volume of MCAs provided to small business is growing rapidly with well over $3 billion in financings currently being provided annually. One reason for their popularity is that MCAs have a flexible repayment schedule which can be advantageous to small business owners and especially those engaged in highly seasonal sales. Since most MCA repayments are based on sales revenue and not a fixed monthly repayment like a bank loan, the repayments for the advance are less when business is slow and higher when sales are robust.

PRIMARY SOURCE OF REVENUE

MCAs are a significant source of revenue for today's brokers and although not true factoring, have now become so popular that all consultants should align themselves with several competitive MCA product providers.

Microloan Programs

Microloans have become an important financing product for budding entrepreneurs worldwide and a product factoring brokers definitely need to become familiar with. These small loans of $500 to $50,000 are shunned by most local banks as being difficult to manage and unprofitable. For factoring brokers, this product provides the perfect opportunity to build solid relationships with loan officers who will gladly refer microloan applications your way. In fact, the product area of micro -lending should be considered "key" when it comes to building solid relationships with loan officers, attorneys, accounting professionals, and other local professionals.

USE FOR ALMOST ANY PURPOSE

Microloans can be used for almost any business purpose including working capital, equipment, inventory, marketing, fixtures, etc. Loan interest rates, of course, are higher than normal commercial bank loans with 10–13 percent being the norm, but are still considerably less than trying to finance a business with credit cards.

There are many providers of microloans nationwide and they can vary greatly from community to community, so you will need to do some online research to locate all of your local resources. Many non-profits, *Small Business Development Corporations* (SBDCs) and *Economic Development Corporations* (EDCs) offering microloans are actually SBA intermediaries, so the place to start learning about micro-lending and the application process is the *U.S. Small Business Administration* at www.sba.gov. The SBA's website explains their popular program in detail and also provides a state-by-state reference list of authorized intermediaries to assist you with finding networking opportunities.

VISIT WWW.SBA.GOV

Getting immersed in your community's microloan programs should be a networking priority as you open your doors. Most providers of microloans require applicants to attend entrepreneur training classes and this is where your earliest small group speaking opportunities may well present themselves.

A NETWORKING PRIORITY

Factoring goes hand-in-hand with small business microloans if the applicant's business is based on B2B sales. In fact, factoring is often presented as an early stage cash flow tool in a start up's business plan, so there is great benefit to booking yourself as a guest speaker at any training classes if possible. Referral accounts from such workshops are initially small with minimal commissions, but they often will grow and multiply exponentially over time.

CAN GROW EXPONENTIALLY

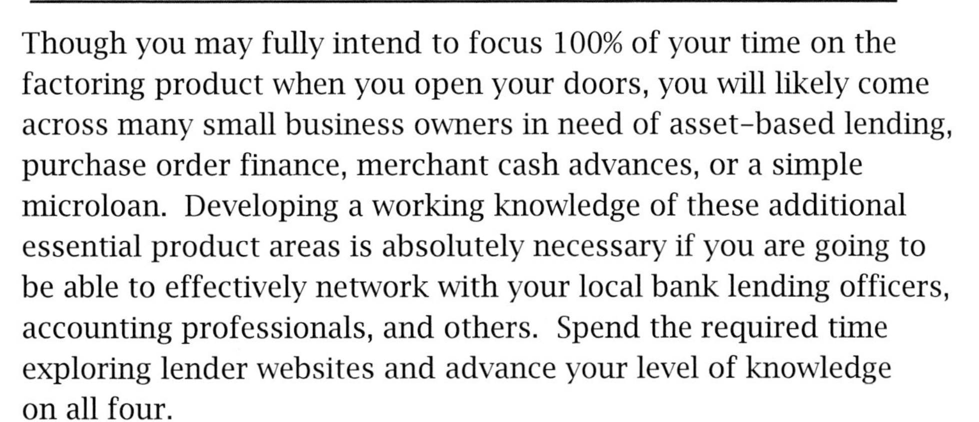

The Bottom Line

Though you may fully intend to focus 100% of your time on the factoring product when you open your doors, you will likely come across many small business owners in need of asset-based lending, purchase order finance, merchant cash advances, or a simple microloan. Developing a working knowledge of these additional essential product areas is absolutely necessary if you are going to be able to effectively network with your local bank lending officers, accounting professionals, and others. Spend the required time exploring lender websites and advance your level of knowledge on all four.

In December of 2013, Elmo McGargle founded *McGargle's Non-Emergency Plus, Inc.,* a medical transport company focused on assisting disabled veterans and senior citizens in need of non-emergency medical transportation (NEMT). McGargle, a disabled veteran himself, financed the company with $5,000 in savings and a $20,000 SBA microloan arranged with the help of local factoring broker, Jon Pendersmite. McGargle used the SBA loan to purchase two used commercial vans which he reconditioned and modified with lifts for wheelchair transport. He also became an approved provider of NEMT through his state's Medicaid office

Partially due to his disabled veteran status, McGargle landed a contract with local county government which had started several programs to assist returning disabled veterans in re-entering community life. One of the programs provided vets with transport to and from the local VA hospital and doctor's offices free of charge. The county was reimbursed for the majority of charges through Medicaid, but due the lengthy time to complete the required paperwork, could only pay McGargle for his transport billings on a net 45 day basis.

The county's new *Disabled Vet Program* soon provided a majority of McGargle's transport business, accounting for nearly 70% of his monthly billings. In fact, he was starting to shop for an additional van and driver to meet the increasing demand. But, McGargle was beginning to see a cash flow problem rear its ugly head due to the 45 days the county needed to pay his billings. McGargle had weekly payroll for his 6 drivers, a monthly SBA loan payment, increasing fuel costs, and also a growing monthly insurance bill to meet state insurance requirements. He realized he needed some type of interim financing program to meet his current cash outflow needs while waiting for county checks to come in. In short, he needed factoring.

Elmo quickly turned to his old friend Jon Pendersmite for assistance. Pendersmite quickly recognized exactly what would be needed, helped Elmo complete a Company Profile factoring application, and then arranged for a conference call with a factor he had been working with for several years. McGargle was billing about $40,000 each month to the county but due to the 45 day payment terms, had outstanding balances of roughly 60,000 each month. During the conference call the factor immediately recognized the opportunity to establish a relationship and forwarded contracts via overnight courier. But there was a small problem. The SBA loan.

When perfecting its loan with a UCC-1 filing, the SBA lender had secured the loan with "all assets" of the debtor. This naturally included accounts receivable and the factor would need to speak with the lender to explore its ability to get a subordination on the accounts receivable. Fortunately, this proved to be no problem since the loan was over 50% paid off and the vehicles would provide more than enough collateral to secure the balance of the loan. **FACTORING COMMISSION EARNINGS: $300 - $400 per month.**

Moneywhistle's **BIG LOADS**

FREIGHT BROKERAGE SERVICE

Polly Sprinklemyer opened *Sprinklemyer and Associates*, a business finance consulting firm in 2011. She began by working only part-time at her new consulting business but by her second year, had begun earning enough commissions from factoring referrals to leave her full time job as a receptionist and focus solely on her growing freelance business finance consulting practice.

Polly had spent most her spare time during the first two years networking and building relationships with CPA's and loan officers. Most she had met at after hours meetups hosted by her local Chamber of Commerce, but she also belonged to a women's civic organization where she had met several good sources of referral. One very important source was Janelle Kneemann, a "special assets officer" at one of the area's larger banks.

Polly learned that special assets officers were put in charge of loan accounts which were "out of formula" and deemed no longer desirable at the bank. This meant Janelle was in charge of finding new homes for loans the bank no longer wanted...a perfect match for Polly and her factoring business.

One day while having lunch with Janelle, Polly was asked to explain a little more about factoring. She gladly did so and Janelle asked Polly if she could come back to the bank with her after lunch to discuss a possible referral.

Janelle's bank had a problem client, *Moneywhistle's Big Loads*, a large freight brokerage operation which was slightly out of formula. Additionally, although the bank already had a $3.5 million credit facility provided to *Big Loads*, they needed more money. Over $500,000 more to be exact, and the bank was not willing to extend additional credit.

At first this looked like an easy factoring arrangement but there was only $3.3 million in accounts receivable and at an 80% advance, there would not be enough to take out the bank's loan. Polly did notice something on the bank's worksheet, however. Some of the customers of *Big Loads* were in Canada and the Canadian receivables, being foreign, were considered ineligible and not included in the loan's credit line formula. The total Canadian receivables were over $600,000. Since the bank was not using these as collateral, they would not have any problem subordinating those invoices to a factor.

Polly quickly set up a conference call with a factor that financed in Canada and an account was set up for *Moneywhistle's Big Loads*. The factor provided temporary financing on the accounts for over 9 months while a new asset-based lender was put in place by Polly. Monthly factoring fees were about $20,000 per month. **FACTORING COMMISSION EARNINGS: $3,000 - $3,500 per month. ABL PLACEMENT FEE $22,500.**

Factoring Construction Receivables

The factoring of construction related receivables is certainly one of the more difficult niche areas of factoring from the transactional standpoint, but one all brokers should become very well acquainted with. Why you say? Because the need for financing in this segment is so great that some brokers can actually focus 100% of their marketing efforts on construction factoring and make an exceptional living. To do so, however, you need to become an expert in all aspects of this important niche area.

SOME FOCUS 100% OFTHEIR MARKETING EFFORTS

First, you need to know that construction factoring provides services to several different categories of prospective clients. And when factors finance in this sector, one size does not fit all. From a product knowledge standpoint, there is quite a bit for brokers to learn.

THREE TYPES OF CLIENTS

When focusing your marketing efforts in the construction sector, you will have three possible types of clients or prospect groups for your marketing campaigns . They are:

- **SUB-CONTRACTORS:** Those actually performing the work on a jobsite and being paid for that work by a General Contractor
- **GENERAL CONTRACTORS:** Seeking to get advances on progress payments made to them by project owners or banks
- **SUPPLIERS:** Businesses that supply materials to the jobsite. This is everything from lumber and trusses to bulk hardware.

Of the three groups, sub-contractors will be your largest market and the easiest to actually interact with. The second most promising group will be suppliers. The general contractors themselves are the smallest group and by far the most difficult to finance. In fact, few factoring brokers working this sector actually market to general contractors.

Factoring Sub-Contractors as Clients

NOTES

The factoring of sub-contractor receivables is the most common in this niche. Here, the invoices being factored are those payable by a general contractor to the sub-contractor for its work on the job. What makes this area difficult? Here are a few risks not typically associated with "plain vanilla" factoring.

- **RETAINAGE:** Most sub-contractor invoice payments are subject to something called *retainage.* Retainage (usually 10% of the invoice face amount) is a holdback the general contractor retains for (sometimes up to a year) to offset poor craftsmanship that may show up well after the sub-contractor has left the jobsite. Because of retainage, all sub-contractor invoices factored are subject to having additional reserve held of 10%. A normal 80% initial advance becomes a 70% or even 65% advance.

10% HOLDBACK FOR RETAINAGE

- **SETOFFS:** General contractors most often enjoy something called *rights to setoff.* This means that an invoice payment for a current job performed may be reduced or "setoff" by a chargeback on a job performed months prior.

- **VERIFICATION:** While the verification process is usually very straightforward in most everyday factoring transaction, it can be problematic in construction. This is because the invoice verifier, in the normal chain of command in a construction deal, is the project manager who will typically be on the jobsite and difficult to access.

- **CONDITIONAL LIEN RELEASE:** Prior to paying an invoice, the general contractor will require a conditional *mechanic's lien release* which protects it from the sub-contractor filing a lien against the job after being paid. This creates some additional paperwork for factors and it can also create a logistical problem since the general contractor will not pay without the release and the release must often be signed in person at the general contractor's offices.

CONDITIONAL MECHANIC'S LIEN RELEASE

Dealing With the Sub-Contractor's General

In most cases, factors will not enter into a sub-contractor factoring arrangement unless the general contractor is an exceptionally strong credit. Additionally, most will only finance those involved with commercial building construction and not residential housing. You should understand, when you submit a sub-contractor construction financing deal to a factor, there will be several difficulties the factor will need to overcome for the deal to get done. These include:

WAIVER OF SETOFF

- **WAIVER OF SETOFF:** The general contractor will have to sign a *waiver of setoff.* This will insure that the invoices purchased by the factor will not be reduced in payment due to a poor past performance of the sub-contractor.

- **NOTIFICATION:** The general contractor will sign a notification requiring payment be made directly to the factor. While this in its own right is not unusual, in construction factoring an arrangement must be in place to provide the general contractor with a *conditional mechanic's lien release* at the time of payment.

- **VERIFICATION:** A reliable method of obtaining solid verification from the project manager or company officer that binds the payment from the general contractor must be in place.

Focusing on sub-contractor factoring deals usually requires the broker be very active with both sub-contractors as well as general contractors in the community and although we will discuss marketing in more depth in a later chapter, this is a segment where holding breakfast or after hours workshops (where both general contractors and subs attend) is very beneficial to building your business.

Sub-contractors are often *paid-as-paid* which means they do not expect to get paid in a set time frame such as 30 days under normal terms of payment, but rather paid after the general contractor receives funds from a progress billing.

Aside from the obvious benefits of factoring for the sub-contractor (getting an early payment advance), there are notable benefits to the general contractor as well. Many sub-contractors can ill afford to be strung out 60-75 or even 90 days before being paid by a general. An early advance by a factor to the sub-contractor can relieve a great deal of pressure on the general to make early payment prior to receiving its scheduled *progress payment.*

PROGRESS PAYMENTS

Factoring General Contractors as Clients

Factoring arrangements where the client is a general contractor are the most difficult and risk prone from the factor's standpoint. Usually, when a general contractor contracts for a job, a payment schedule will be created so the general contractor receives periodic cash draws at certain stages during the construction process. Such cash draws are termed *progress payments* and are the result of an invoice called a *progress billing* being generated and forwarded to a paying bank or the project owner.

PROGRESS BILLING

When certain criteria or tasks have been accomplished on a normal construction job, the general contractor submits an invoice for a progress payment. When factoring a general contractor, it is this progress payment invoice they wish to factor. The primary problem when factoring invoices from a general contractor for a progress billing is that the payment for that invoice from the bank or project owner can be reduced or set off due to *mechanic's liens* filed by any unpaid sub-contractors.

Though they vary from state to state, all states now have some form of *mechanic's lien law* which protects property owners, construction professionals, and suppliers from non-payment when they have performed services to a job site. Under these laws, a *notice to owner* is typically filed in the form of a lien or pre-lien on the jobsite and will not be released until the sub-contractor is paid.

MECHANIC'S LIEN LAWS

Mechanic's liens work to the benefit of factors when financing sub-contractors as they put additional payment pressure on the general contractor. Conversely, they work against the factor and represent significant additional risk when financing a general contractor. If a factor purchases a progress payment invoice from a general contractor who has made no payments to subs on the job, the factor is at risk of receiving a reduced payment on its invoice as the bank or property owner pays the sub-contractors so mechanic's liens will be satisfied and removed.

OFTEN PAY SUBS DIRECTLY

Factors will usually offset risk of sub-contractor mechanic's liens by paying the subs directly from the general contractor's advance on the progress payment. In return, the factor will be provided a lien release by the sub. Clearly, when financing a general contractor's progress billing, the factor must know all sub-contractors and suppliers who have worked or provided services on the jobsite. This can be a difficult task and is one reason construction factoring fees for general contractor factoring arrangements tend to be slightly higher than for most other factoring segments.

SLIGHTLY HIGHER FEES

Suppliers to Contractors as Clients

Suppliers selling to general contractors represent the easiest group to factor in the construction industry. This is because they enjoy the safety of the same mechanic's lien rights if goods are delivered to a specific job site but are seldom subject to retainage or rights to setoff as with a sub-contractor.

A general contractor will most often have 30-60 days to pay for goods (hardware, lumber, windows, appliances, cabinetry, etc.) based on their credit arrangements and the factoring facility will usually be based only on the general contractor's creditworthiness. There are no conditions of offset (other than occasional issues of damaged goods) to be dealt with nor difficulties regarding invoice verification due to a hard to reach site manager.

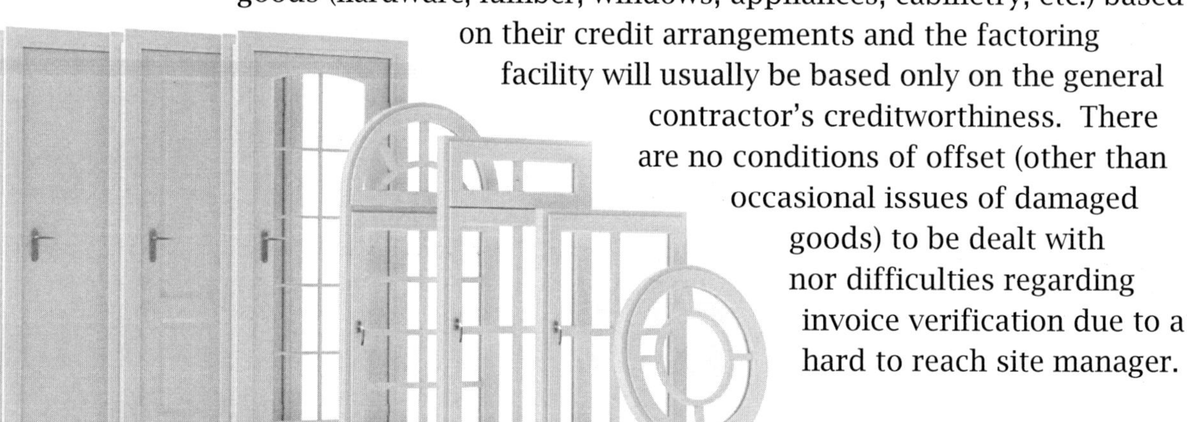

Performance Bonds

When underwriting general and sub-contractors, performance bonds often come into play. Basically, on jobsites where invoices are being factored, general contractors may be required to have a bond in place. Sub-contractors cannot have a bond in place. This is because a bonding company can theoretically "prime" the factor's payment if the sub-contractor decides to walk away from a job and the bonding company hires a replacement to finish the work.

PRIME THE FACTOR

Types of Sub-Contractors That Commonly Factor Their Receivables

Construction is an enormous segment of the economy with hundreds of specialty sub-contractors operating within its borders. Freelance brokers practicing in cities or service areas of size can often focus 100% of their time in this area and make a good living. To do so, however, you will need to align yourself with several good factors specializing in the construction industry and learn their programs inside and out.

SOME BROKERS FOCUS 100% OF THEIR TIME

Types of sub-contractors that will often utilize factoring to smooth out their cash flow include:

- **site preparers**
- **well drillers**
- **directional boring companies**
- **landscaping companies**
- **roofers**
- **framers**
- **drywall installers**
- **crane and backhoe operators**
- **utility contractors**
- **electricians**
- **demolition companies**
- **steel erectors**
- **paving companies**
- **construction clean-up companies**
- **lumber distributors**
- **truss builders**
- **tile / carpet installers**
- **plumbers**
- **many others**

Staffing & Temp Services

The staffing industry represents a primary market for factors and brokers should always maintain a keen watch for new staffing companies opening their doors in the community. As you are aware, one of the primary reasons for factoring is to fund weekly or bi-weekly payroll. No industry has a greater need for payroll financing than staffing.

Staffing companies come in many shapes and sizes, often specializing in a particular niche. There are medical staffing companies, construction staffing companies, those that specialize in accountants and bookkeepers, companies that provide computer programmers, hospitality staffing, and the list goes on and on.

INTENSE PAYROLL NEEDS

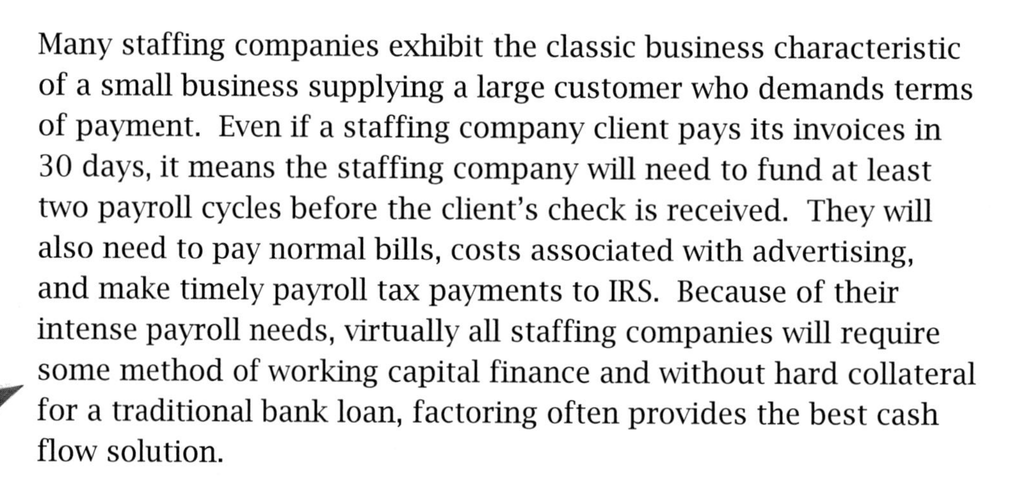

Many staffing companies exhibit the classic business characteristic of a small business supplying a large customer who demands terms of payment. Even if a staffing company client pays its invoices in 30 days, it means the staffing company will need to fund at least two payroll cycles before the client's check is received. They will also need to pay normal bills, costs associated with advertising, and make timely payroll tax payments to IRS. Because of their intense payroll needs, virtually all staffing companies will require some method of working capital finance and without hard collateral for a traditional bank loan, factoring often provides the best cash flow solution.

Factors will generally provide significant additional services to even the newest of staffing companies. In many cases, factors completely run the back office, allowing the staffing business owner to focus fully on marketing and business development. Such services include:

- **Advances of cash against invoices**
- **Integrated accounting with programs such as *QuickBooks***
- **Invoice mailing and processing**
- **Time card management and payroll check printing**
- **Credit checking and collections**
- **W-2 and 1099 document preparation & tax return support documents**

Factoring Agricultural Receivables

Factoring trade receivables linked to food and the sale of goods and services in the agricultural sector can be very difficult for factors. In fact, many factors have a strict policy against factoring "anything that grows". Still, as with all difficult niche areas, a small group of factors have developed a process or formula which reduces the risk to the extent that financing can be performed confidently.

The problem with financing invoices related to foods or goods that are perishable (fresh produce, meats, flowers / plants, etc.) is, of course, spoilage. This is one reason that factors who do provide such services in this "fresh" niche, will usually advance at a much lower rate, holding additional reserve for spoilage.

PACA LAWS

Another major problem when factoring agricultural products is something called the *PACA Laws* (*Perishable and Agricultural Commodities Act*). PACA Laws are similar to the mechanic's liens found in the construction industry and provide growers with the rights to file financial damage claims if they are not paid for shipments and are victimized by buyers and merchants. A grower not paid for its shipment of produce, can file a claim with the PACA Trust and if valid, will have the right to "prime" a lender for payment upon an invoice. For example, a grower not paid for tomatoes shipped to a ketchup manufacturer, will have the right to claim invoice payment from a grocery store chain which purchased the ketchup. If a factor or similar lender is financing the manufacturer and expecting payment upon the chain store's invoice, it could suddenly find itself in second position for payment due to the PACA claim.

Another issue that makes financing foods even more difficult is the ability to fully ascertain what is and is not covered by PACA. Certain foods may be exempt from PACA if processed in a certain way. Others may not. Such ambiguity elevates financing agricultural products to a level of high risk and an area where only very specialized lenders with significant PACA experience will tread. When performing lender research as an industry broker and building your lender database, make certain you locate at least one or two factors who provide services in this important but difficult niche area.

Government Receivables

EXCEPTIONAL RISK WITH GOVERNMENT RECEIVABLES

On the surface, factoring government related receivables might seem like a perfect factoring opportunity. After all, there is little risk that most governmental entities will go bankrupt and those in trouble are well known in advance. In reality though, factoring receivables payable by federal, state, and municipal entities represents an exceptionally risky financing loaded with all sorts of dangers for factors and lenders. Brokers marketing to government contractors will immediately find the need to build a relationship with a factor specializing in this problem niche area.

THE FEDERAL ASSIGNMENT OF CLAIMS ACT

The *Federal Assignment of Claims ACT of 1940* was enacted to facilitate a method of financing government contracts during World War II. Referred to as *FACA Laws*, the act sets forth regulations which outline methods for lending institutions to take assignment of government payments due government contractors.

Unlike the normal system of notification provided by Article 9 of the Uniform Commercial Code, the FACA Laws present a set of different rules and regulations for a lender to establish legal assignment of accounts and payment thereon. These rules and processes include specialized release forms, the need for approval with notarized signatures, and a *notice of assignment* form unique to the Federal Government. In some cases, granting an assignment to a lender will actually require a new contract to be drawn between the government and the supplier.

ASSIGNMENT FOR STATE CONTRACTORS

EVEN LARGER MINEFIELD

Factors experience significant additional risks associated with misdirected payments when financing entrepreneurs providing goods or services to the federal government. An even larger minefield, however, can exist when dealing with states and occasionally even municipalities.

In many states, an assignment is only valid if authorized by a specific officer of a particular state agency and there is little commonality in requirements from state to state. Factors providing financial services to clients engaged in state work must have a very expansive knowledge of the various state laws regarding assignments. For example, Minnesota prohibits a lender from filing suit against it if the state should make payment to the wrong entity after valid notification, thus completely voiding the safety that notification normally provides.

From the freelance broker's standpoint, marketing to small and minority business owners engaged in bidding for government contracts is a very good niche. Many small business owners, awarded exceptional contracts because of their minority enterprise status, subsequently have a difficult time fulfilling the award due to working capital limitations. Factoring can alleviate a great many of the payment problems associated with such small business awards. Make certain you include several government receivables factors in your lender database.

CONTRACTS DUE TO MINORITY STATUS

Real Estate Commissions

The factoring of commissions due agents from sales of real estate is a relatively new area of specialization for certain factors. While it slightly breaks the standard rule of B2B only non-consumer related transactions, it is looked upon as a valid factoring niche by the factoring industry anyway.

FAST GROWING SEGMENT

In the real estate industry, this type of factoring transaction is referred to simply as a *commission advance* and has become quite common in large real estate agencies. It is very beneficial to sales people who often experience many peaks and valleys regarding income. Commission advances help to smooth out income droughts when sales are slow. Real estate agent commission advances are now one of the fastest growing segments of the factoring industry.

OVER 10% OF SALES NOW BENEFIT FROM A COMMISSION ADVANCE

In most cases, the commissions earned by real estates sales people are paid at the time the transaction closes or shortly thereafter. In other instances, and especially in large transactions, commissions earned can be scheduled for payment over longer periods of time due to multiple closings. A typical example of this is when a large piece of vacant land is sold to a developer and closings will occur periodically, as the development expands and opens different sections. It is not unusual for such property transactions to close in 3, 4 or even more installments with the commission due the salesman paid at each individual closing. It is estimated that over 10% of all current real estate sales now benefit from a commission advance.

Real estate commission advance factors will advance on agent commissions earned from the sale of residential properties, condos, commercial properties, industrial, and raw land. Advance rates can run from 80% to 90% depending on the factor and the transaction and advances can be made upon closings scheduled up to 90 days in the future with even longer advances made on a case-by-case basis. Once capped at just $10,000, today's real estate commission advance providers now have virtually no advance limits on qualified transactions.

Fees charged on commission advances are a bit more expensive (roughly double) than those charged on traditional factoring, evidencing the elevated risk of financing such one-off spot transactions. Recipients can expect to pay 5%-6% for 30 days with longer advances being commensurately higher. Still, this is a much appreciated financial tool for many agents when funds are scarce.

Most large real estate franchises already have commission advance agreements in place for their franchisees and this is not a particularly attractive area in which to market for factoring brokers. Still, there are some opportunities available for setting up arrangements in larger non-franchise operations with 10 or more agents. Brokers will additionally need to explore which commission advance factors work with brokers on a referral basis. Many do not.

Trucking & Freight Bill Factoring

NOTES

The factoring of trucking receivables is currently the largest sector by volume of the domestic factoring industry with roughly 17% of all factoring in the U.S. involving freight bills. This area has proven to be very "fertile ground" for niche factors and also for large factors with specialty freight bill factoring departments.

LARGEST SECTOR OF THE FACTORING INDUSTRY

Factoring in this popular area is actually very similar to normal advance / reserve factoring and includes high advance rates and expert credit and collections services. In a typical freight bill factoring transaction, the over the road hauler will pick up and deliver the goods to a customer. Instead of submitting the invoice to the customer, the freight company will submit it to the factor who will provide an advance of cash usually within 24 hours.

When advancing against freight bills, factors often provide "above and beyond the call of duty" services and benefits such as:

PROVIDES FUEL CARDS

- **FUEL CARDS:** for the purchase of diesel fuel along the route
- **FUEL TAX REPORTING:** assistance in report preparation
- **DISCOUNTS:** on fuel, tires and truck maintenance
- **STATE AUTHORITY FILING:** assistance in filing for their state authority with the FMSCA (Federal Motor Carrier Safety Admin.)
- **APPLICATION MONITORING:** assistance with all permitting
- **FREIGHT BROKER SERVICES:** assist their clients in finding return shipments after delivery

Because of its size, freight bill factoring is a very competitive niche area with some of the industry's lowest rate structures. Factors servicing this area are aggressive buyers and factoring services are generally available to almost anyone in the industry regardless of size or time in business. The many additional services provided to the sector means that factoring can be an exceptionally attractive financing alternative for start-ups and small operators.

VERY COMPETITIVE NICHE AREA

Third Party Medical Receivables

Every year, hospitals and physicians provide billions of dollars in services to patients with a large portion of billing for such services being submitted to medical insurance companies and governmental entities such as Medicare / Medicaid. It is not unusual for a doctor with even a small practice to have in excess of $500,000 tied up in such receivables. For a broker initially exploring this industry, its important to distinguish between third party medical receivables and normal healthcare receivables.

- **THIRD PARTY MEDICAL RECEIVABLES:** represent "claims" paid by an insurance company , HMOs, PPOs, Medicare / Medicaid, or similar state agency for medical services performed on an individual. No workman's comp. claims are allowed
- **HEALTHCARE RECEIVABLES:** are invoices of those companies billing physicians, labs, hospitals, etc. for goods delivered or services performed.

HIGH QUALITY HEALTHCARE RECEIVABLES

Healthcare receivables are normally very high quality with debtors being hospitals, labs and relatively large, creditworthy companies. Third party medical receivables are just the opposite, being paid by insurance and quasi-insurance companies where offset and claim denial are common. Such third party medical receivables are exceptionally difficult to finance and require a specialty factor with a very highly trained staff.

ADVANCE RATES OF 60% OR LESS

Because insurance companies are notorious for making payments which are substantially less than a claim (billing) or sometimes even making no payment at all, the risks involved in financing third party medical receivables runs high and justifies much lower initial advance rates. Rather than the normal advance rate of 80% or higher in a standard factoring transaction, advances of 55% or lower are common when purchasing third party medical receivables.

Few medical receivables finance companies limit their financing to receivables alone and brokers should know many provide such services as:

- **Bankruptcy and Debtor-in-Possession Financing (DIP)**
- **Revolving and Non-Revolving Credit Lines**
- **Acquisition Finance**
- **Letters of Credit**
- **Medical Equipment Leasing**

For most brokers, the third party medical receivables business represents a relatively difficult sector to penetrate unless you have some history in the medical industry with very robust networking opportunities. You certainly do need to be aware of this type of financing, however, and also make certain you add at least one third party medical receivables factor along with several healthcare factors to your lenders database.

DIP Financing

FACTORING A BUSINESS IN BANKRUPTCY

Factoring is one of the few methods of financing readily available to small business owners struggling to re-establish their business through a Chapter 11 bankruptcy or reorganization. While such "restructuring" of debt is commonly provided through the asset-based lending community for larger business entities, small business operators are only served by the factoring community.

Bankruptcy factoring or "DIP" financing (Debtor-In-Possession), is a unique niche area of factoring which requires a high degree of due diligence and additional legal processes not found in everyday factoring transactions. Because of these additional requirements, all factors do not provide service in this unique niche area. DIP factoring is an area that most brokers ignore. It is one, however, that can generate significant annual revenue for those that become familiar with its inner workings.

When underwriting a prospective client for DIP factoring, the factor will look closely at the cause of the insolvency to determine if a factoring arrangement can solve the problem. If factoring can address the cause of the business's problems and, under normal circumstances, help return the business to profitability, a factoring arrangement may be established.

RELIEF FROM THE AUTOMATIC STAY

To establish a DIP financing arrangement, the factoring agreement must be approved by the federal bankruptcy court. If approved, the factor will be granted relief from something called the *automatic stay,* which is part of federal bankruptcy law and provides protection for debtors (and customers) from collections during the period of the bankruptcy. Since factors will be purchasing invoices and collecting upon them, they must be granted relief from the legal limitations placed upon them by the automatic stay. Additionally, factors will be purchasing assets (invoices) of the insolvent business and all such asset sales must be approved by the bankruptcy court.

For small business owners, access to DIP financing through factoring during troubled times can literally make the difference between survival and a complete business liquidation. Very few business owners, however, are aware of this critical financing option available through factoring. In many instances, factoring can help to return the business to profitability and provide the means for the business to meet its obligations owed to previous lenders and creditors.

CHECK THE LOCAL NEWSPAPERS

LOCATING DIP DEALS

DIP deal financing opportunities are overlooked by most brokers yet it is often very easy to find a lead or two. When a business is involved in bankruptcy, that bankruptcy is a matter of public record and while few personal bankruptcies are considered news, business bankruptcies often are. By occasionally reading the public records posts in your newspaper, you may come upon a golden opportunity for factoring a DIP deal.

Spot Factoring

Occasionally, a factoring transaction will be requested by a prospective client which involves the purchase and advance upon what amounts to a one-of-a kind invoice of unusual size or payment terms. An example of such a transaction would be when a small products distributer, billing perhaps $30,000 per month, suddenly finds itself faced with a single, unexpectedly large $100,000 order from a very creditworthy retailer who demands 60 day payment terms. The distributor is currently not factoring its invoices, but doesn't want to decline the order simply because it cannot afford to ship that much product and wait 60 plus days to get paid. The small business owner clearly needs some creative financial assistance on this particular order. The problem's solution involves something called *spot factoring.*

SPOT FACTORING

Most spot factoring requests simply involve one or two very large invoices with extended payment terms. About one half of all factors will entertain such spot factoring requests. Others will not, simply due to the increased risks involved by having "all eggs in one basket" so to speak. When spot factoring transactions are approved by a factor, the client can expect to pay a much higher fee rate than it would under a normal factoring arrangement.

EXPECT TO PAY A HIGHER RATE

Spot factoring should not be confused with "seasonal" factoring where a company, because of the seasonal nature of their business, requires financing 3 or 4 months out of the year. Companies dealing in holiday products such as Christmas decorations, lights, holiday related clothing, foods, etc., often require factoring for the holiday season when sales spike but not during the rest of the year.

SEASONAL FACTORING

For brokers, the commission earned on such singular transactions will be minimal so its certainly not worth your time and effort to market for such transactions. However, many such "one shot" accommodations eventually become excellent long term factoring arrangements with clients factoring all of their invoices once they see the cash flow benefits of factoring and the ease with which an arrangement for factoring can be put in place. When you are building your lenders database, make note of factors that mention spot factoring on their websites and create a record for one or two.

Micro-Factoring

ACCEPTING INVOICES AS SMALL AS $1,000

Micro-factors are small factors often servicing their local community. In many cases, micro-factors are successful industry brokers that have made the leap to financier. Most regular factors will not accept clients factoring less than $15,000 per month with exceptions granted only on a case-by-case basis. Micro-factors, on the other hand, are true mini-financing entrepreneurs often accepting transactions as small as $1,000 while they expand their service areas and learn the financing side of the factoring trade.

LIGHT VERSION INVOICE TRACKING SOFTWARE

As brokers develop their business, they will naturally be exposed to various contracting documents required to create factoring arrangements. They will learn how to search the UCC and file a security interest. They will often have the capability of creating accounting spread sheets, advance schedules, and other documents in programs like *Microsoft Excel* or similar software products. Alternatively, they may even opt for one of the less expensive "light" versions of professional invoice tracking factoring software available from industry providers.

Micro-factoring is a natural area of business expansion for a small percentage of factoring brokers who want to make the transition from broker to factor. To make this move, however, you will need a reasonable amount of capital and some very specialized training in both the administrative and legal areas of the business.

ADDITIONAL TRAINING AND LEGAL ADVICE

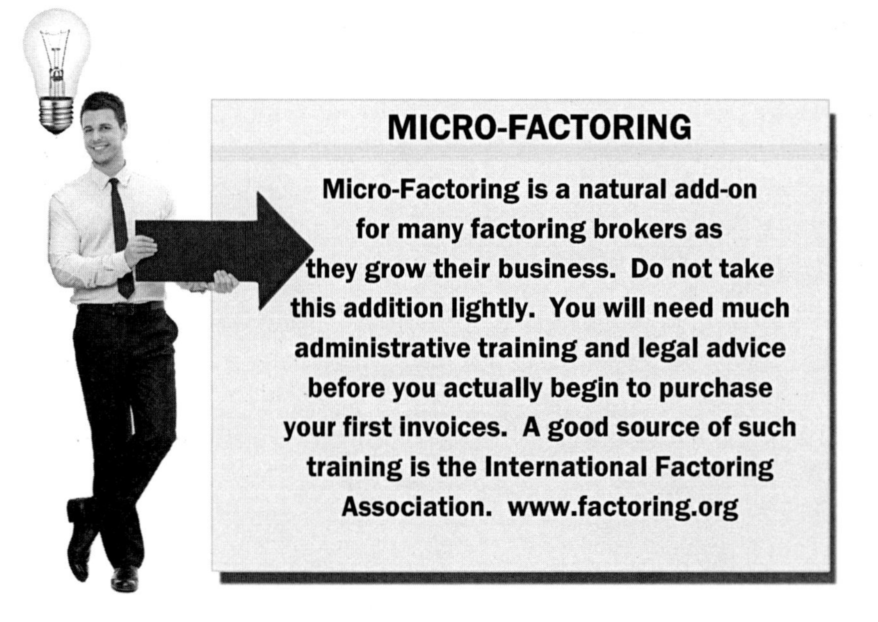

Micro-factors tend to work closely with community banks and local small business incubators who welcome such mini-financiers. Micro-factors who will entertain investment in new and very small entrepreneurial enterprise can represent an excellent source of referral for banks and others who cannot finance such small, under collateralized, invoice-based transactions.

MAKE THE SMALL DEALS HAPPEN

Micro-factors can be a valuable resource but are also difficult to locate since they primarily only advertise in their local markets. Factoring brokers should be on the lookout for such entrepreneurs, however, since they can often make the small deals happen.

Poultry and Meat Packers

SIMILAR TO PACA LAWS

Similar to the PACA Laws which protect growers and agricultural products producers, *PASA Laws* (*The Packers and Stockyards Act*) protect the financial interests of poultry producers, livestock ranchers, and swine producers from non-payment and deceptive practices by dealers, distributors, and livestock brokers. The *PASA Laws* were originally passed in 1921 to curb certain monopolistic practices of the major meat processors of the time. The provisions and reach of the act have been modified and amended over the years.

Important to factors and factoring brokers is the statutory trust provisions introduced by amendment in 1976 which protects cash sales made between producers and packers. Under PASA, producers that remain unpaid for sales up to 30 days post delivery can file a written notice to the U.S. Department of Agricultural and submit a PASA claim. Factors who have advanced on the receivables of meat processors and packagers can be "primed" regarding the payment of invoices from supermarket chains and food products manufacturers. For example, a dog food manufacturer using meat bi-products in its product and neglecting to pay for such bi-products, can have its invoices from sales to pet stores effectively "levied" by the Department of Agriculture and the PASA Trust. A factor providing financing services to the dog food manufacturer and advancing on invoices payable by its customers can be left without payment due to such a PASA claim.

International Factoring

Domestically, factors provide well over $100 billion in commercial finance annually to American business owners. On a comparative basis, that's just a very small fraction of the volume of factoring services provided worldwide. For example, the United Kingdom, a relatively small nation, generates roughly double the factoring volume of America. International factoring is BIG BUSINESS.

HOW DO I GET PAID?

U.S. small business owners have one primary concern when selling to a cross-border buyer. That is: *how do I get paid?* In reality, those involved in international sales must deal with three primary risks:

⇒ **CUSTOMER CREDIT RISK:** dealing with the difficult task of determining the creditworthiness of a buyer located in a foreign country.

⇒ **CURRENCY RISK:** risks of being paid in a currency other than the U.S. dollar whose value can fluctuate.

⇒ **POLITICAL RISK:** those risks associated with the stability (or lack thereof) of foreign governments.

ELIMINATION OF NON-PAYMENT RISK

For experienced exporters, there are various methods of reducing or sometimes completely eliminating those risks when choosing a method of payment for international sales including:

⇒ **CASH IN ADVANCE:** a common method of payment but the least attractive to a customer and one which will limit sales.

⇒ **LETTER OF CREDIT (LC):** one of the most secure methods of payment but very complex, expensive, and one which will draw down the credit lines of a customer.

⇒ **DOCUMENTARY COLLECTIONS (DC):** less expensive than letters of credit and similar in some ways, documentary collections lack the implicit guarantees of an LC.

⇒ **OPEN ACCOUNT:** the most advantageous to the customer and one that will enhance sales, open account treats international customers identically to domestic customers.

From purely a sales standpoint, selling on *open account* is by far the most advantageous method of conducting business but also the most risky. Without cash up front or the guarantees associated with an LC, domestic sellers may find themselves hiring a collections attorney in a foreign country. There are, however, many ways to reduce the risk inherit in *open account sales* and one of the easiest and most popular methods is simply to employ international factoring.

How International Factoring Works

A COMPLETE FINANCIAL PACKAGE

International factoring offers a complete financial package which combines finance, credit risk protection, currency risk protection, bookkeeping, and collections. Almost all international transactions are conducted on an advance / reserve and non-recourse basis to the exporter, thus protecting it from non-payment due to an importer's bankruptcy or insolvency.

There are always four parties to any international factoring transaction. They are the:

- **EXPORTER**
- **IMPORTER**
- **EXPORT FACTOR**
- **IMPORT FACTOR**

4 PARTIES TO AN INTERNATIONAL FACTORING TRANSACTION

Because of the growth of international factoring and the size of the many factors today specializing and providing services in this important niche, it is now quite common for the export factor and import factor to be one in the same.

In an international factoring transaction, an advance will be made to the exporter through the export factor just as in any common domestic transaction. The export factor will work directly with the import factor often adhering to something called the *General Rules of International Factoring* or GRIF, for short.

60 / 40 SPLIT

The import factor acts as guarantor on the transaction and it is the import factor's job to establish the creditworthiness of the buyer (importer). In some cases, the import factor may purchase *credit insurance* to alleviate non-payment risk. Because of the additional risk associated with the import factor's role, factoring fees are typically shared on a 60/40 basis with the import factor receiving the larger share of 60% and the export factor receiving the lesser amount of 40%.

Many small and mid-size factors now routinely provide some services on an international level. Large international factoring transactions are often handled by members of the international factoring organization, *Factors Chain International.*

80% OF ALL INTERNATIONAL TRANSACTIONS

Factors Chain International

Factors Chain, established in 1968, is a global network of factors engaged in international transactions. With its recent (2016) partnership with the former *International Factors Group* (IFG), Factors Chain now boasts over 400 members operating in 90 countries. Its members are responsible for over 75% of all global factoring and approximately 90% of all cross-border international factoring transactions.

For those brokers intending to focus heavily in the manufacturing and distribution sectors, having a strong working knowledge of export factoring can set you apart from all competition. You can find out more (including available FCI courses) at http://fci.nl

As cross-border trade continues to expand throughout the world, the area of international factoring will continue to grow exponentially, since it provides a readily available "simplistic" approach to such finance. Compared to *letters of credit,* international factoring is much less complex as well as being less expensive when dealing with the problems associated with payment on export sales and especially small (under $1,000,000) sales.

Freelance brokers marketing in the manufacturing and distribution sectors will certainly run into questions regarding exports and how to insure payment upon them. And although the SBA and EXIM Bank have some excellent options for large transactions, international factoring is rapidly becoming the financing method of choice for small and mid-size business owners due to its non-recourse features as well as its inherent simplicity.

BOTH IMPORT AND EXPORT FACTOR

Because of the unique fee sharing arrangement between export and import factors, its advisable for brokers having client referrals who are heavily involved in exporting to work with an international factor of size who can play the role of both export and import factor. Not only will this simplify the transaction, but it will also insure that the broker gets paid a commission on both sides of the financing.

Accounts Receivable Credit Insurance

Accounts receivable insurance or *trade credit insurance* is an insurance product which insures the accounts receivable of a business against loss due to the insolvency or bankruptcy of a customer. Though it is most often associated with international transactions where the credit history and rating of a buyer is unknown to the seller, trade credit insurance is just as commonly used in domestic transactions.

Trade credit insurance can be used to insure a single large sale but is more often employed as a *blanket* or *master* policy insuring a group of account debtors. The policy owner (the exporter or seller), is provided with policy limits per customer by the insurance company which details the maximum exposure to loss allowed per customer. A rider to the policy is typically used to include new customers as sales are made.

USED IN CONJUNCTION WITH EXPORT FACTORING

Credit insurance is sometimes used by an exporter in conjunction with an export factoring transaction. The insurance tends to lower the cost of factoring since the factor is no longer exposed to a possible loss due to insolvency or bankruptcy of a debtor. While a credit insurance policy will guaranty payment, it is not a stand alone method of finance and will not provide an advance of cash like factoring.

TAKE THE QUIZ

Chapter 3 Quiz

1. A quasi-factoring product used to finance personal injury lawsuits is a ____________

   A. personal injury advance
   B. pre-settlement legal advance
   C. attorney's fee advance
   D. none of the above

2. Loans made to businesses primarily based on the strength of the business's balance sheet are __________

   A. asset-based loans
   B. financial statement loans
   C. equipment loans
   D. all of the above

3. One of the most difficult loans for a young company to obtain is a (an)_________________

   A. asset-based loan
   B. financial statement loan
   C. factoring loan
   D. equipment lease

4. Asset-based loan providers are primarily interested in the liquidation value of a collateral rather than financial statements.

   A. True
   B. False

5. Asset-based loans typically provide_________________

   A. an 80% advance on accounts receivable
   B. a 50% -60% advance on inventory's fair liquidation value
   C. a revolving line of credit
   D. all of the above

6. To detail the available credit line, asset-based lender will periodically prepare a (an)____________________

   A. accounts assignment schedule
   B. accounts collection schedule
   C. borrowing base certificate
   D. all of the above

TAKE THE QUIZ

7. A method of financing the manufacturing of goods so they may be delivered against a valid order is____________________

   A. asset-based loans
   B. factoring
   C. purchase order finance
   D. mobilization loan

8. An amount (often 10%) held back by a general contractor as security for poor performance by a sub-contractor is__________

   A. a setoff right
   B. retainage
   C. holdback
   D. mechanic's lien

9. *FACA Laws* provide for an agricultural grower to file a claim in the event it is not paid for produce shipments.

   A. True
   B. False

10. Roughly 17% of all factoring transactions involve____________

   A. freight bills
   B. construction
   C. staffing payroll
   D. real estate commissions

ANSWERS TO THESE AND OTHER QUESTIONS CAN BE FOUND IN THE BACK OF THE GUIDE

ANATOMY OF A BROKERED DEAL

Submitting Your First Deals

NOTES

Being a factoring consultant means you need to acquire a broad base of knowledge regarding your product areas. Textbook definitions of financing terms is great but as you begin to develop leads and prospects, the inevitable "How does it work?" question will be asked a thousand times. So, in order to answer confidently, you need to know a little more about how you submit business to a factor, how your submission is underwritten, and how the subsequent daily operations necessary to provide your client with factoring services work.

Some great news here is that submitting a prospective client to a factor almost could not be simpler. Once you've located an interested business owner through your marketing efforts, there will only be one completed form necessary to submit your deal. That is called a *Company Profile.*

COMPANY PROFILE

A Company Profile (download PDF in the *Learning Lab*) is a 2-3 page document which provides some "quick look" background info for a factor to determine whether the client and the client's industry is suitable for the factor's portfolio. Or in other words, is it a match?

As an independent broker, you have absolutely no contracting or additional document duties. In fact, almost anything else you provide at submission will simply be duplicated when the factor begins its own due diligence process and underwrites the deal. Your freelance brokering business is strictly one of lead generation and qualifying. Nothing more and nothing less.

Where to Submit Your Deal

Once you have a completed *company profile*, you will need to call upon your newly acquired broker skills to determine exactly where to send it for financing. As discussed in the last chapter, there are hundreds of what we would term "plain vanilla" factors who will always be happy to look at your deals. If your deal involves a *niche area* of factoring, such as construction, you need to make certain you send the deal to a factor who provides services in that specialty industry area.

Analyzing the Company Profile

ANALYZE THE PROFILE

When you receive a completed *company profile*, you will need to perform some initial analysis of the submission to determine if it is a valid deal that deserves your attention or one which represents an impossible task. As you know, asset-based finance is all about collateral. If a true collateral exists, there is probably a way to finance it. If no collateral exists, there are few options for funding and factoring certainly isn't one of them. Below are some items to check, areas of concern, and questions to ask your prospect based on an initial profile submission.

- **LEGAL DESCRIPTION:** View the legal name of the business and check it at the Secretary of State's website in the client's state of operation or incorporation. If a corporation or LLC, it should be "ACTIVE". If not, tell the client the status must be updated to "ACTIVE". While not 100% necessary for you to do this, this addition to your submission package makes it and you look a little more professional to the factor. Print the results of your legal description search and include it along with the *company profile* when you submit the deal.

- **BANK LOANS OUTSTANDING:** As you know, your factor will require a senior secured 1st lien position in accounts receivable in order for a factoring arrangement to be put in place. If bank loans are evidenced on the *Company Profile*, talk to your prospect to determine the purpose of the loan. Does it involve real estate, vehicles, equipment, or is it a line of credit?

  If the loan is a business line of credit, it is likely that the bank has a *blanket lien* with "all assets" of the business pledged to secure the loan. If a loan balance is not included on the Company Profile, ask the business owner the approximate loan balance and what the loan is for. If you are in a state that provides free UCC searches, you can pull the UCC filing and view the collateral statement.

  MANY ARE UNAWARE

  Additionally, do not be surprised if an outstanding loan is not referenced at all on the Company Profile. Many business owners are unaware that a UCC Financing Statement has even been filed on what they may consider a "personal loan" by their bank. Here again, if the business resides in a state where access to the UCC database is free, always search the database for filing information. If no filings exist, there are no loans outstanding which have a senior lien on accounts receivable.

  In many states, although you can search the UCC for filing information, you cannot view the image of the filing nor see the actual collateral liened without paying a fee. If you cannot tell, just reference the loan and the filing on your submission. The factor will pull the record and find what collateral secures the loan.

  TAX LIEN PAYMENT PLAN INFORMATION

- **TAX LIENS OR PAYROLL TAX ARREARAGES:** If a tax lien is present or tax payments are in arrears, find out the balance involved and also if a *payment plan* with the IRS is in effect. Tax liens are not necessarily deal breakers, but must be dealt with in a way that eliminates the ability of the IRS to levy the payments due from purchased customer accounts and *prime* the factor. Tax liens can also be searched in every state and usually for free.

EVEN IF THESE TWO (EXISTING LOANS AND LIENS) AREAS ARE LEFT UNCOMPLETED ON THE COMPANY PROFILE, YOU SHOULD ALWAYS SEARCH THE UCC FOR EXISTING LOAN FILINGS AND DO A TAX LIEN SEARCH IF POSSIBLE. The factor will quickly perform both once you submit the deal, but if you have access to free lien searches, its good policy to do both a UCC search and tax lien search.

Common Submission Mistakes

As you should now know, deal submission in factoring is deceptively simple but there are several very common mistakes made by "newbie" brokers and they almost always involve identifying the type of financing needed. As a new freelancer, you will understandably be excited when you get your first completed company profiles, but don't let your excitement allow you to make any of the following mistakes.

AVOID SIMULTANEOUS SUBMISSIONS

- **SIMULTANEOUS SUBMISSION:** As an expert consultant, you always want to refer your clients to the right factor and get them a "good deal". Never, however, fax or email simultaneous submissions to different factors at the same time. Simultaneous submission are very much frowned upon in the industry and if discovered, will cause most factors to simply walk away from the deal.

  Brokers should choose a factor carefully and then let that factor do its initial underwriting to either accept or decline the deal. The industry is very competitive from a fee standpoint and if you have chosen a factor in the right niche area and your client qualifies, there will be no need for any subsequent submissions.

MOBILIZATION FUNDING

- **KNOW THE DIFFERENCE BETWEEN FACTORING AND CONTRACT FINANCE:** We've already discussed this in the previous chapter but here it comes again. The biggest mistake made by industry neophytes is the inability to know the difference between a doable FACTORING deal (which always involves an invoice) and CONTRACT finance which involves no immediate invoice but the need for what is termed *mobilization money* to get a project started.

Contract finance is similar to purchase order finance except for one major distinction:

NOTES

- **Contract Finance** usually involves a small business who is the beneficiary of a contract to provide a service.
- **Purchase Order Finance** usually involves a small business who is the beneficiary of a purchase order to deliver goods.

Both involve the need for some form of mobilization funds, however contract finance involves additional risks that are unacceptable to almost all lenders since there is initially no collateral (no invoice or goods). See example below.

> **Jim Smith owns a landscaping company and receives a $30,000 contract to provide landscaping services for a local bank. The local bank has agreed to pay for the service in 30 days from completion.**
>
> **To provide the service and fulfill the contract, Jim needs $7,500 to purchase trees, shrubs, and to rent a backhoe. In other words, he needs *mobilization funds* to begin the work. He comes to Jonas, a local factoring broker he recently met at a Chamber of Commerce meetup for funding.**
>
> **Jonas explains to him that what he needs is *mobilization funding*, not factoring. Once the job is completed and an invoice is then generated for $30,000, it could easily be factored if required due to extended terms of payment given to the bank. But until the service is performed, there is no collateral in the form of a valid invoice for a lender to provide financing.**

Almost all "newbie" brokers make the mobilization funding mistake, usually because they think there might be something they're missing in the deal and it can somehow be done. So, they run it by a factor just to see. Mobilization funding deals will always be declined unless the funding is based on a valid invoice. Query the prospect to find out if he or she has other invoices where the work has been performed but payment has not been received. Perhaps these can be substituted and used to provide the needed funding.

Deal Submission Step-by-Step

The following is a practical step-by-step guideline that will help you submit your first deal to a factor. It includes items you should review prior to submission.

- **COMPANY PROFILE:** Fax or email a company profile to your prospect and have them completely fill it out and sign it. Once completed, have them return it to you via fax or email. Make certain you have filled out the "Broker Info" on the profile so your factor is aware of who submitted this deal. (Company profiles in PDF format are available for download in the Learning Lab)
- **ACCOUNTS AGING REPORT / CUSTOMER LIST:** Your factor will want to review the names of the primary customers of the prospect for credit analysis. If possible, have your prospect send a customer list with addresses or/and an *accounts receivable aging report.* An A/R aging report shows all of the currently outstanding invoices of the business. If you do not provide this, the factor will request it from the prospect during underwriting anyway.

REVIEWING THE PROFILE

- **REVIEW THE COMPANY PROFILE:** Review the profile for completeness and take notice if the prospect listed any current loans or any tax liens outstanding. If these are present, call the prospect to get additional information. These are potential deal breakers and its best to get to the bottom of them early. If there is a:

  Tax Lien Outstanding: Find out the approximate dollar balance of the arrearage and if a payment plan is in effect. Factors must have a senior lien on accounts receivable to provide financing and an IRS lien subjects the accounts they purchase to possible levy.

  Prior Loan Outstanding: If a prospective client has an existing business loan from a bank or similar lender, it is almost a certainty that lender has filed a lien and security interest upon the business assets. If possible, find out how the loan is secured (what is pledged for collateral) by accessing the UCC database.

- **LOCATE A FACTOR:** If the company profile is completed and there does not appear to be any "deal breakers" evident, locate a factor in your database that you feel is suitable to handle this type of transaction (i.e. industry or deal size). Contact the factor and ask to speak to someone in business development that can handle a "brokered" transaction. You will be connected to a principal of the firm or to a BDO (Business Development Officer).
- **INTRODUCE YOURSELF:** Introduce yourself and tell your contact that you have a deal you would like to submit. Ask if they would please email a *Broker's Agreement* for you to execute.
- **REVIEW THE BROKER'S AGREEMENT**: There are basically three (3) areas of primary importance on any standard factor's *Broker's Agreement.*

  Commission Rate: this will usually be either 10% or 15% percent of the factoring fees earned but there are also some "exotic" structures out there. Beware of broker agreements that pay based on "funds employed" as those pay based on the advance rate and may be less than a standard industry rate.

  10% - 15% COMMISSION RATE

  Residual Life-of-Account Payment: The vast majority of all factors pay for life of the account. A very few pay for only one year. Make certain yours pays for account life.

  No Charge-Backs: There should be no provision for charge-backs against the broker in the event the factor-client relationship fails.

  If the *Brokers Agreement* is acceptable (and virtually 100% are), sign the agreement and return it to the factor or BDO. Always have a signed Broker's Agreement in hand before you send in the company profile. This tends to be a very honorable industry, but there are always exceptions.

  HAVE A SIGNED BROKER'S AGREEMENT IN HAND

- **SEND IN YOUR DEAL & PAPERWORK:** Once you have a signed agreement, send in the company profile and other documents if any.

INTRODUCE AND STEP OUT

- **CONFERENCE CALL:** On the cover page, ask about the BDO / factor's availability for a conference call with the prospective client. Work with the times provided and set up a conference call between yourself, the prospect and the factor. On the call, introduce the prospect to the factor or BDO. Then step out, listen, and learn.
- **DEAL FINALIZATION:** If the factor accepts the deal, you are done. The factor will close the deal, issue contracts, and begin the financing. There is nothing more for you to do other than collect commission checks.
- **BACK TO WORK:** NOW...go find another five prospects!

Initial Underwriting by the Factor

The initial underwriting by the factor will be accomplished very quickly, typically in just a few hours. After your submission and successful conference call, the factor will forward a *Terms and Conditions Agreement* (sample in the Learning Lab) to the prospect. This short, one or two page document outlines the provisions of the proposed factoring agreement. If acceptable, the prospect will return the terms sheet with signature. The factor will then quickly perform a:

- **Corporate Records Search:** to validate the correctness of the business identity
- **Uniform Commercial Code Search:** checking for existing liens against accounts by an active lender
- **Tax Lien / Judgment Search:** to check for existing business or personal liens
- **Criminal Background Check** to investigate felony convictions for the owner or owners of the business

VERY CREATIVE FINANCIERS

If any of the above four items are present, they are potential "deal busters" if they cannot be addressed properly or rectified. Factors are very creative financiers, however, and in many instances such problems can be addressed satisfactorily.

The Factoring Agreement

Once the client has signed the *Terms and Conditions* letter and a UCC and tax lien search concludes no liens exist, the contracting can be finalized with the client signing a standard factoring agreement (commonly called a *Master Purchase and Sales Agreement*). This agreement, among other things, will define and set forth the fee arrangement, authorize notification of assignment to customers, and define rules and guidelines for the factoring arrangement. It will also address events of default and their remedies.

STANDARD FACTORING AGREEMENT

Filing the UCC-1 Financing Statement

The *Master Purchase and Sales Agreement* authorizes the factor to file its UCC-1 Financing Statement, perfecting its security interest in the accounts receivable of the client. The UCC-1 is filed at the Secretary of State level in the state of the client's incorporation. Prior to making the first advance, the factor will normally conduct a second UCC search to make certain the filing is correct and senior in its lien position.

Noticing the New Customers

As you know, *notification of assignment* provides the mechanism for a lender (factor) to take control of the invoice payments made by the customers of the new client. Once notified by the factor of its security interest in accounts receivable and the payments thereon, the client's customers are now obligated to pay the factor and no other entity. This means they will no longer pay the client.

NOTIFICATION OF ASSIGNMENT

Notifying the client's customers will usually be done two ways.

- **By Letter:** This will be a friendly but formal letter which addresses the assignment and the new "remit to" address of the factor or the factor's lockbox.
- **By Legend:** During the advance, a "notice of assignment" legend will be attached to the invoice. The factor may additionally have the client change the "remit to" address on the invoice template of its accounting software.

Selective Notification

In some instances, a client may wish to factor only the invoices of a select group of customers and not all customers. For example, the client may have several large customers which take 30-45 days to pay their invoices, creating a cash flow hardship, and requiring factoring for a method of remedy. But the client may also have some smaller customers who pay their bill in under 10 days. Factoring for such customers is simply not needed or required.

Such *selective notification* and financing is generally acceptable to most factors. The fact that certain customers are not being factored, however, does not affect the factor's security interest in all accounts. Should an event of default occur, the factor can quickly notify such "non-factored" account debtors and require them to begin making payments directly to the factor as well.

Events of Default

The factoring agreement will define *events of default* which are those occurrences that can bring the factoring arrangement to an immediate and abrupt halt. Primary among those is something called *misdirected payments* or simply *collection.*

IMMEDIATE TERMINATION

Obviously, when a factor purchases an invoice and notifies the customer regarding the assignment of the payment, the factor expects to be paid. *Collection* occurs when a client receives a misdirected payment from a customer on a purchased invoice in error, after valid notification of assignment has been made, and then does not immediately turn that payment over to the factor. *Collection* by a client represents civil theft and is justification for immediate termination of the factoring agreement...or worse!

Contract Term

AUTOMATICALLY RENEWS

The factoring agreement will define the contract term which will usually be one year. In most cases, the factoring agreement will automatically renew each year unless the factor is notified to the contrary by the client.

The First Advance of Funds

When a the new client returns the signed contract, the factor will begin processing the first advance of funds. Most clients will have existing invoices already outstanding which can be included in this advance, provided they are less than 30 days old and the factor can achieve a valid notification prior to the invoices being paid. The client will add additional new invoices to its existing invoices and combined, they will be used to create the first advance of funds.

INCLUDES OUTSTANDING INVOICES

The factor will create something called an *advance schedule* which:

- **lists the purchased invoices consecutively by invoice number**
- **totals their amount**
- **multiplies the total by the factor's advance rate (typically 80%)**
- **reduces that total amount by any deductions (such as a wire transfer fee)**
- **determines the net advance amount to be wired to the client's business bank account.**

CREATES THE ADVANCE SCHEDULE

The Verification Process

As you already know, factors are purchasing a piece of paper (an invoice) which is presented to them as valid by your client for goods delivered or services performed. Prior to an advance, factors will validate the invoices being purchased through *verification.*

The Advance of Funds

When the factor's advance is finalized, it will be faxed, emailed or electronically made available to your client who will check the advance for accuracy and then sign the advance document. Once the advance is prepared by the factor and then signed by the client, the funds are disbursed within just a few hours through direct wire transfer to your client's business checking account.

FUNDS ADVANCED

Processing Collections

With the invoices now purchased and customers noticed to make payment directly to the factors, payments will begin to be received. In some cases, payments will come directly to the factor's business address. But more likely, they will be received at a *lockbox*, which is a special post office box operated by a bank.

As payments are received, they are posted into the factor's invoice tracking software and a *collection report* is created. The collection report will provide all of the information regarding each invoice paid by the check, the customer's check number, the advance report number related of the invoice purchase, the advance date, the payment date, and the total fees earned by the factor.

COMMISSION REPORTS

Brokers Commission Reports

The commission report for the referring broker is based on the total collections received during the month for all referred clients. Most factors provide broker commissions monthly with the start date being the first of the month and the end date being the end of the month. The commission report itself is based on the sum of the various client collection reports generated during the period.

There are several standard formats used by factors for their brokers' reports but most will display both total purchases and total collections for the period. The *collections* will show the factor's fees earned and then multiply that amount by the broker commission rate. The *purchases* made during the month will provide the broker with a snapshot of what fees will be earned in the near future.

The client does not see the referring broker's monthly commission report. It is also important to note that the factoring fee rates charged to a client are not affected by the fact is was referred by a broker. Brokers are simply looked at as an internal sales expense and cost of doing business, the same as if the client was generated by one of the factor's in-house BDOs.

Broker Commissions, Fees, and Bonuses

OK! Now for the good part...the MONEY! Freelance brokering is a very, very lucrative occupation and the commissions and referral fees paid are extraordinary. And, there are many types of commissions depending on the financial product. Here, however, we will focus strictly on those associated with factoring.

Commissions paid to independent factoring brokers tend to be relatively unique in the commercial finance industry. This is because they are:

- **RESIDUAL:** This means they are paid on a continuing recurring basis each month based on collections
- **LIFE-OF-ACCOUNT:** This means you will receive such residual commission payments for as long as your referral continues to use the factor's services

LIFE-OF-ACCOUNT COMMISSIONS

This commission style is also common for purchase order finance referrals but most other product areas pay a one-time fee in "points" (a percentage of the loan amount) much like a typical real estate loan.

Referral commission fees paid to brokers are most often 10%-15% of the fees earned by the factor. This range depends on the factor, the size of the account, the factoring arrangement's fee structure, and the amount of continuous business you, as a broker, send to a particular factor. Factors will also run periodic bonus programs or sales contests where commissions can occasionally be as high as 20% of the factoring fees earned.

FACTOR'S BONUS PROGRAMS

Broker commissions are paid monthly and you will usually receive a check during the first week of the calendar month for commissions generated the previous month. When first submitting a deal for financing, it will often take two (2) months or more before you receive your first commission check. This is because your fees are based on the factoring fees which, in turn, are a function of collections. Factors must purchase and then be paid on invoices before service fees can be tallied and broker commissions paid.

TAKE THE QUIZ

Chapter 4 Quiz

1. A "generic" application used by many new industry brokers is called a_____________

   A. company profile
   B. client profile
   C. financing application
   D. none of the above

2. Brokers can download generic company profile forms at_________________

   A. the IACFB Annex
   B. The Learning Lab
   C. Campus IACFB
   D. all of the above

3. When a client completes an application as a corporation or an LLC, a search of the Secretary of State's corporate records should show an _____________ status.

   A. filed
   B. revoked
   C. active
   D. franchised

4. A lien on a security filing which takes "all assets" of a business as collateral is referred to as a _________________

   A. Total lien
   B. Blanket lien
   C. Full security lien
   D. Full Recourse lien

5. Simultaneous submissions are considered normal when submitting deals.

   A. True
   B. False

6. One of the biggest mistakes all new brokers make when submitting their first deals is knowing the difference between purchase order finance and ____________________

   A. factoring
   B. floating lien finance
   C. contract finance
   D all of the above

TAKE THE QUIZ

7. If possible when submitting a deal, include a (an) ____________

   A. IRS lien report
   B. collections report
   C. accounts receivable aging report
   D. all of the above

8. The normal commission rate for factoring submissions is ______

   A. 5-10 percent
   B. 10-15 percent
   C 15-20 percent
   D 20-25 percent

9. On factoring submissions, brokers receive commissions that are _______________

   A. life-of-account
   B. residual
   C. paid in points
   D. both A and B above

10. The client factoring agreement is also called the _____________

   A. Discount and Advance Agreement
   B. Sales Advance Agreement
   C. Master Purchase and Sales Agreement
   D. None of the Above

ANSWERS TO THESE AND OTHER QUESTIONS CAN BE FOUND IN THE BACK OF THE GUIDE

GETTING READY FOR BUSINESS

Pre-Opening Tasks

NOTES

As we said, factoring brokers come in many shapes and sizes. Many will simply be individuals seeking to supplement their income from a current profession such as bookkeeping, tax preparation, insurance, financial planning, etc. Others will be looking forward to a more career-oriented industry participation on a full-time professional level. So, how you set up your business and business office will naturally depend on your personal business goals. Regardless of those goals, however, you will at least need the following:

WHAT ARE YOUR GOALS?

- A well thought out work space (home office or commercial space)
- Computer and printer (desktop, laptop, or both)
- Software (several specialty software products)
- Telephone & answering system (hard line preferable with cell backup)
- Apparel (business suits for both men and women)
- Vehicle (dependable and visually acceptable)
- Storage space (and lots of it)

All of the previously mentioned are business essentials and if you are seeking to enter the industry on a truly professional basis, there are few benefits in being overly frugal here. You should also avoid, however, going completely overboard and burying yourself in debt. Simply get the best you can afford. After you land your first deals, you can upgrade these basics as required. You will however, need all in some form or fashion to get started on any kind of an operational basis.

Creating Your Business Identity

One of the first hurdles you will need to tackle is choosing a good name for your new consulting business and there are several important business name characteristics to consider including:

- **PROFESSIONALISM:** You are not about to open up a neighborhood lemonade stand but rather a very prestigious financial business as a highly compensated freelance consultant. When choosing a name for your consultancy, think very professional, not gimmicky.
- **NAME LENGTH:** You will be using your business name on business cards, letterhead, advertisements, and your website. In many cases, exceptionally long business names can cause unforeseen marketing problems such as when you are placing column width classified ads.

CHECK DOMAIN AVAILABILITY

- **DOMAIN AVAILABITY:** If you haven't already done so, you will very shortly be purchasing a website domain (your address on the internet) and here, shorter is always better. When exploring business names, you should immediately check to see if a domain is available that either matches your business name or one that represents a shortened version of it. It should also be available with the TLD extension of .com You want to avoid extensions such as .net, .biz, .us, etc.

CHECK FOR TRADEMARKS

- **CHECK FOR TRADEMARKS:** Make certain your name does not infringe on a registered trademark. This is easily done at the website of the U.S. Patent and Trademark Office. http://tmsearch.uspto.gov

- **CHECK YOUR STATE FILINGS:** Businesses operating in any name other than that of the owner will be required to file or register that name with the state. They may be registered as a corporation, LLC, partnership, or simply as a DBA (doing business as). Check to see if your business name choice is already active and not available. If you decide to incorporate or form a partnership, get some legal and/or tax advice from a competent professional. Most brokers operate as an LLC, but that election may not be the right one for you. Get advice!

Using a Business Name Generator

BUSINESS NAME GENERATOR

When choosing a business name as a consultant, one good option is to simply use your own name much like an attorney, CPA, or similar professional. For example, if your last name is Smith, names such as Smith Business Capital, LLC or Smith Capital Associates, LLC are more than acceptable. But if you're trending towards something a little more creative, you can get some great ideas from an online *Business Name Generator.*

Using your favorite internet search engine, type in " free business name generator" and you will find a host of these useful tools available to you. With a *business name generator*, all you do is type in a word or two that you want your business name to contain and the generator works its magic, displaying thousand of combinations and suggestions. Many generators will not only generate suggested business names, but will also check to see if that particular domain name is available for your company website.

COMBINATIONS OF KEY WORDS

Before using a business name generator, it's a good idea to do a little searching on the internet for financial websites first, so you can select a few "key" words or combinations you might like in your business name. Many will give you great ideas to help get started. Financial companies tend to use names that project strength and trust.

Again, using your favorite search engine, select "DMOZ Finance". This will display DMOZ's directories of various types of finance companies including factors. Take some time to visit sites and research names and combinations.

Registering Your Website URL

Once you have settled on your business name, you need to immediately reserve your URL This will be your website's "www" address on the web. On the internet, there is no room sharing. Only one entity can have a particular address (called a URL). If the one you want is already registered, you will need to select another. Even though you have the legal right to use a business name in your state, the internet is a world stage. Someone, somewhere, may already have registered the domain you want. To check to see if a particular domain is still available, you can go to www.checkdomain.com.

Here are a few rules, helps and hints in choosing your URL:

MOST IMPORTANT PART OF A DOMAIN

- There are several parts to a URL. Only two, however, are of significant importance to you. The most important part is called the "label" or simply "domain". That is usually your business name or some abbreviated version of your business name such as "smithassoc" or "atlantabizcap". Its the part that goes between the dots in your URL.

ALWAYS SELECT .COM IF AVAILABLE

- The second most important part is called the TLD which stands for "top-level domain". This is the part that goes after the second dot and is most often "com". So a typical domain my be something like "smithassoc.com".
- The third and fourth parts are of little importance to you. The "http" part stands for Hyper Text Transfer Protocol and is used to identify a particular location on the internet. The "www" part is a sub-domain that tells the world your particular location is the World Wide Web.

ONE MISTAKE EVERY SEVEN KEYSTROKES

When selecting your website's domain, always remember that shorter is better. The average web visitor makes a mistake of some kind every 7 keystrokes. Although the label portion of a domain can legally be as long as 63 characters, having such a long domain is just asking for trouble. A very long domain means many potential visitors (clients) may never find you. So when it comes to your website's domain, shorter is always better. Make it as short as possible while still maintaining your business identity.

Another reason for shorter domains is you will be using them in classified ads and other important marketing materials. In some cases, fitting long domains into available ad space will require fonts of such a reduced size, that they are almost illegible.

UNINTENDED CONSEQUENCES

Also be aware that when shortening your domain, it is easy to generate completely unintended (and occasionally unsavory) words as you abbreviate. Once you think you have created a good domain and one which is available for registration, step back and look at what you've created. Your domain will be imprinted on every type of marketing support item you create such as brochures, flyers, business cards, etc. If you make an embarrassing mistake when creating your domain, it can cost hundreds or even thousands of dollars to correct later.

Setting Up Your Business Email

Now that you have a business name and web address, you need to set up a business email address. Here again, you have several choices. Some good...some bad.

SEND / RECEIVE BUSINESS EMAIL

- **PERSONAL EMAIL:** This is usually a very bad choice. Avoid it!
- **FREE BUSINESS:** Often you can get a free email address through providers such as *Gmail* or *Yahoo* that relates closely (or exactly) to your business name.
- **EMAIL FORWARDING:** This is usually FREE or very inexpensive and is provided by your domain host. It is a "mask" of your personal email and is receive only.
- **DOMAIN HOST BUSINESS EMAIL:** This is a true business email associated with your domain name usually of the POP3 or IMAP variety. Domain associated emails are provided by your domain host and will look something like *info@mydomain.com* or *joe@mydomain.com*. This type of business email is a true send / receive email address and a great marketing tool. It is very inexpensive and we will talk a little more about how to use this email for marketing in the next chapter on business development.

Choosing an Office Location

Another early decision you will need to make is where you will operate from and just what type of office you will have. Here, you really have three choices.

- **HOME OFFICE:** Utilize a current home office or establish a new one in your residence
- **EXISTING COMMERCIAL OFFICE:** Use an existing office you already use
- **NEW COMMERCIAL SPACE:** Lease or rent office space

MOST COMMON OFFICE CHOICE

For most new freelancers just starting out, the most common choice for initial operation is a home office. This is simply because it is both convenient and will almost always come with few "visible" costs. With a home office, you will certainly save on rent, utilities, time spent commuting, and probably some furnishings. This is all good when start up capital is at a minimum. A home office does, however, come with its own set of problems.

INVISIBLE COSTS OF A HOME OFFICE

As an independent freelancer, YOU MUST BE PRODUCTIVE and home offices are famous for providing distractions which can significantly impact your performance and overall industry success. Such negative attributes of a home office can be looked at as the "invisible costs" of working from home. And, such costs can be significant. So if you have decided to work from home, they must be overcome.

Work From Home Productivity Killers

NOTES

After selecting a location and laying out your home office, try to avoid the following pitfalls and productivity killers when working from home.

- **Distractions:** Avoid distractions such as the need to do a load of laundry or vacuum a floor. Install a highly visible wall clock in your office and avoid the rest of the house during your set hours of operation.

- **Poor Dress:** Shower and dress for work every day. This does not mean you have to put on a suit and tie. But, don't attempt to work in your pajamas either.

- **Boredom:** If you find yourself getting bored or losing interest in work, take a break. Head to a coffee shop for "intermission". As you will learn in the later chapter on marketing, you should always try to schedule a networking opportunity around lunch. Get some breathing space.

DUNGEON EFFECT

- **The Dungeon Effect:** Locating a home office in a room without a window is a sure way of killing productivity. Natural daylight is a productivity enhancer and the best type of lighting for your office. If you have a window with a view, it will provide you with a way to take an occasional "brain break". You will need additional task lighting, of course, for cloudy days and after hours work. Stick with "natural daylight" shades of light and avoid harsh types of lighting that produce an uncomfortable glare.

BACKGROUND NEWS PROGRAMMING

- **Television:** Background televisions (for news only) can offer small benefits by providing you with mini-breaks, but limit listening to "news only" type programming. Catch up on world events during office hours. You need mini-breaks at least every hour.

Moving to Commercial Office Space

There are tremendous benefits to be had for factoring brokers when operating from certain types of commercial space. You will likely need to sit down and have a serious talk with yourself, however, before making such an expensive plunge. Considerations will include:

- **CASH FLOW:** Can you afford rent, utility expenses, new furniture, and still pay your current living expenses?
- **SKILLS:** Do you have or are you determined to develop the necessary skills required to succeed as a career broker so you can justify such a move and long term expense?
- **DETERMINATION:** Do you have the determination and perseverance to succeed as a factoring consultant on a truly professional level?
- **FULL TIME COMMITMENT:** There is no real reason to opt for commercial space unless you are focused on the business full time. If you are simply operating part time, the home office route is probably right for you.

FULL TIME COMMITMENT

If you have doubts about any of the above, confine yourself for the time being to your home office. Wait until you have landed your first deals, have some residual factoring income coming in each month, and can comfortably afford the additional expense which comes with a move to commercial space.

Gauging the Benefits of Commercial Space

Let's start out by saying this: a home office provides a perfect launching pad for almost every factoring freelancer. It's easy. It's convenient. It's cheap. But if you've decided your residence can no longer provide you with what you need for productivity or if you find that not having meeting space or an assistant is crippling your marketing efforts, you may need to look at the commercial option. If located properly, good commercial space can lead to walk-in business. And, one or two average walk-in clients per year can completely cover the expense of your commercial space and more.

WALK IN CLIENTS

Choosing the Right Location

NOTES

Having a commercial address will add enormous amounts of credibility to even the smallest consultancy. Your status as a true industry professional will be enhanced dramatically. Not all commercial space is created equal, however, when it comes to your unique area of consulting. Before you sign on the dotted line, here are some tips, ideas and good recommendations for what will benefit you the most as a freelance factoring consultant.

BANKS WILL OVERBUILD

- **BANK SPACE:** When a local bank builds a new building they will always overbuild for future expansion. Until they actually need the space, it will be leased. Such space is perfect for your business. The opportunities for networking and relationship building with loan officers will be endless. If you are looking for commercial space, look for space within a bank. You simply cannot do better than this.
- **ACCOUNTING FIRMS:** Space adjacent to large accounting firms runs a close second to banks. CPA's and accountants can send a great deal of business your way once they get to know you. Its unlikely you will find space within the premises, so look for space next door or in close proximity to a large accounting firm.
- **EXECUTIVE SUITES:** Executive suites are a group of small to mid-size offices housed within a large commercial building. They provide not only a private office, but come with extensive "common" amenities. These amenities will include a reception area with receptionist, conference rooms, lunch area, bathroom facilities, business services room, and an adequate parking area. An executive suite can be an excellent choice if located in the "mover and shaker" part of town with good networking opportunities.

CONFERENCE ROOMS AND COMMON AMENITIES

- **LAW FIRMS:** Fourth on our list would be law firms involved with business law. All the same benefits apply and especially those firms heavily involved in corporate bankruptcy filings and reorganizations.

When choosing a commercial space for your brokering business, one of your primary considerations should be networking and walk-in traffic. Gauge what networking benefits and walk-in opportunities this particular location has to offer. For example, locating your office near or adjacent to small business assistance organizations such as the local SCORE office or a local small business incubator can be a real goldmine for referrals and prospecting. As you build relationships with the staff of such organizations, the opportunities to participate in workshops and educational seminars will be never ending.

INVESTIGATE LOCATIONS

So the rule here is this. If you decide the time has come for commercial space, don't just lease a cheap "anything". Spend some time investigating the best opportunities for a new location. A few extra hundred dollars a month is a very small price to pay for the right location if it leads to a bonanza of networking opportunities, referrals, and walk-in traffic.

Designing the Perfect Business Card

With your business name, business address, web address, and email address in hand, you can now have your business cards printed. Do not take business card design lightly. Business cards are a very powerful, yet inexpensive prospecting tool if designed correctly.

Your business cards should be printed on a quality white or cream colored stock. No wild colors and nothing flashy. They should scream out "I'm a professional". But now comes the good part.

In marketing, there is an old adage that states:

Prospecting is all in the questions.
Sales is all in the solutions.

And nothing could be more true. Make certain your card includes a list of product areas. When someone receives your card, you want them to ask: "*What's factoring?*"

You want a business card that makes the receiver ask questions about you and your business. Questions you can provide answers to. Questions that lead to excellent relationship building opportunities. And your business of factoring broker is perfect for this powerful marketing tool, if your business card is properly designed.

Productivity Tools You Will Need

Now that you have an identity and an office, its time to start creating or setting up the productivity tools you will need when you open your doors and begin your business development efforts. Some can be considered optional if you are going to farm out certain work, such as the production of your brochures, for example. These productivity tools include:

CRM: AN INDISPENSABLE MARKETING TOOL

- **COMPANY WEBSITE:** From your first day you will need a well designed company website.
- **WEBSITE ANALYTICS:** This is free and used to track responses to your business website's various pages.
- **EMAIL MARKETING SERVICE:** Used to manage your e-lists for newsletter and bulletin distribution.
- **A CONTACT RELATIONSHIP MANAGER (CRM):** This is a completely indispensable tool used to manage your lists, marketing campaigns, and relationship building processes.
- **BROCHURES & FLYERS:** You will need at least one quality brochure when you open your doors. Flyers and brochures can be created "on the fly" as you develop particular marketing campaigns.
- **ENVELOPES, REPLY ENVELOPES, AND LETTERHEAD:** Envelopes (#10), and reply envelopes (#9) are a must for general correspondence. Any mid-grade stationary will due, since you will be printing this as letterhead using your own computer when required.
- **WORD PROCESSOR OR PUBLISHER SOFTWARE:** You will naturally require some version of word processing software such as *Microsoft Word* or *Publisher.*

Your Virtual Office: Setting Up Your Consultant Website

WEBSITE IS CRITICAL COMPONENT

Of the many tasks which must be performed prior to opening your doors for business, setting up your business website is probably the most important. There is no option here. For anyone operating as a consultant, part-time or full-time, a business website is required. And you should not wait until well after you are completely up and operational. Way too many lead-generating activities are tied to your website, so it needs to be published and available for viewing well before you pass out your very first business cards.

What Your Site Should Contain

There are all types of websites. They can be very professional and laid back or they can feature audio, video, and all sorts of interactivity. And, they can be expensive to construct. But, there's good news here. For factoring brokers and commercial finance consultants, your business website does not need to be complex. In fact, a great professional website for consultants is a relatively simple affair. The pages your site should contain include a (an):

- **INTRODUCTION:** also known as a *Home* or *Index Page.*
- **PRODUCTS:** a page for each of the five "core" product areas (factoring, asset-based lending, purchase order finance, merchant cash advance, micro-loans).
- **CONTACT:** a page with your phone, fax, email address, etc.
- **APPLICATION:** a page containing an online application, a downloadable PDF application, or both.

ALWAYS INCLUDE A SQUEEZE PAGE

- **INVITATION:** sometimes known as a "squeeze page", this is a special marketing page used in conjunction with direct marketing and especially direct mail marketing.
- **REFERRAL:** referrals will be a big piece of your business and you will need a page which promotes them.
- **FAQ:** a *Frequently Asked Questions* page with answers to some of the most commonly asked questions regarding factoring and your other products.

Other Features Your Site Should Contain

In addition to pages, there are several features your business website should contain.

- **NEWSLETTER SUBSCRIBE FORM:** Publishing a newsletter is a very potent lead-generation tool and you should make it easy to subscribe with a short form right on your site.
- **OFFERS:** Your website is like a funnel and gathers leads from your *offers*. You must always have some form of offer on your site that visitors can request. Offers can be a FREE report or white paper, a case study, short booklet, etc., but an offer of some kind must always be present.

- **CALLS TO ACTION:** Every page in your website should contain a *call-to-action*. It might be as simple as a "contact us" link for more information or it might be a request for your current offer.

What Your Site Should Not Contain

We'll talk more about how to use your site for business development and the importance of your invitation page (squeeze page) in the Learning Lab. For now, get your site up and running. But when doing so, there are several things you should avoid during the building process. These include:

NO POP UPS

- **POP UPS:** 95% of web users report a negative or very negative experience regarding sites having pop ups. They can easily block the view of important content. NO POP UPS!
- **ADS:** Though allowing ads on your site can generate a little revenue, the last thing you want is to have a visitor click on an ad and leave your site. NO ADS!

NO LINKS TO OTHER VENTURES

- **LINKS TO OTHER BUSINESS VENTURES:** Many factoring brokers operate multiple businesses. It is not unusual for such active mobile creatives to have a website for each venture. Resist the urge to link them. NO LINKS!

Optimization Your Site for Search Engines

After you have published your site, it is likely you will receive multiple emails from various *search engine optimization* (SEO) companies who, for $500 or more, will optimize your site for a higher ranking on search engines. You should probably avoid such companies at all costs.

WEBMASTER TOOLS

There is little mystery on how to optimize your site for search engines. We can't go into all of the tricks of the trade here, but *Google* tells you exactly how to do it in their published *Webmaster Tools and Guidelines* which are available to anyone. Proper use of page titles, page descriptions, and headings (H1 and H2 tags) generally does a pretty good job of basic SEO.

Page titles and metatag descriptions of each page are very important and the use of a little common sense here goes a long way. If you have set up your consultant business in Miami, Florida, for example, don't just title a page; *Factoring for Your Small Business.* Make the title something like; *Small Business Factoring Services in Miami.* Although there are no geographic boundaries for factoring brokers when it comes to website marketing, try to focus your site's attention on your local market if possible. That way, if a small business owner in Miami is typing in "*factoring services Miami*" in a search box, your site is much more likely to be displayed early in the page rankings.

Also, its very important to understand the primary function of your website. Your site is published to support your inbound and outbound marketing functions, not to generate leads on its own simply due to its existence. If it turns in a few quality prospects for factoring every few months due to searches, consider that a welcome marketing bonus.

IMPORTANCE OF BACKLINKING

An important component in your site's search engine ranking is also backlinking. The more internet links which point to your site, the higher your ranking will become. This reflects on the importance of authoring short articles on factoring and small business finance.

Adding Analytics to Your Website

One of your primary marketing tasks as a consultant is list building and driving traffic to your website, where visitors can download or subscribe to an offer. Wouldn't it be nice to be able to gauge the effectiveness of such marketing campaigns almost immediately? Well you can. You simply need to add a website analytics program such as *Google Analytics.* https://google.com/analytics

Google Analytics is website analytics service that tracks and reports the traffic to your website's pages. It is a "fremium" service with basic subscription being free and then offering additional add-on features for a slight fee. It is the most widely applied analytics service on the internet, being used by approximately 50% of the top 1,000,000 visited websites. One of the best features about *Google Analytics* is its online training programs. This is a complex feature, no doubt. But you can learn to use all of its many benefits in just a few hours thanks to the excellent online training tutorials provided at the *Google Analytics* website.

With analytics installed on your website, you will be able to accurately measure visits to the site and even to particular pages as a result of your various marketing campaigns. For example, if you create a direct mail campaign using a list of staffing companies in your area and offering a FREE report or FREE case study, you can measure the number of visits to your website's *squeeze page* and also see how many downloaded the actual report. With the statistics in hand, you can then initiate a "warm call" follow-up program to contact this new response list or even use the list for invitations to an upcoming workshop or seminar.

MEASURE VISITS TO YOUR INVITIATION PAGE

Probably the most important reason to have a good analytics program installed on your website is simply to determine which marketing campaigns are working and which are not. With analytics, for example, you can test a direct mail program's effectiveness by just investing in a small sample mailing of perhaps 250 pieces. If the analytics report shows the results of the small mailing were successful, you can then feel confident launching a larger campaign.

TEST DIRECT MAIL PROGRAMS

Your Email Marketing Service

OPT-IN ONLY

An email marketing service company is simply a business that provides what the name implies, bulk email services. An email marketing service helps to organize your email campaigns and contact lists. Its very important to note, all email marketing services require the names you add to your list to be "opt-in". Or in other words, your lists cannot contain email addresses you simply collected, purchased, or picked out of thin air.

FORM BUILDER AVAILABLE

All email marketing companies will have a suite of ready-to-use templates for your newsletters and bulletins. They are very easy to edit and modify. Of even greater importance, your email marketing service will have a "form builder" for your website. The form builder will generate the html code necessary to display an opt-in form for visitors to complete. Simply paste the code into your site's html and you will have an opt-in form which will automatically add a subscriber's name to a pre-defined list you've created. You can also add an automatic "Welcome" email which will be sent to your website visitors right after they subscribe.

Even though you may not publish a monthly e-newsletter on day one of operation, you need to start building e-lists of visitors to your website specifically for that purpose. An email newsletter does not carry the weight of a print newsletter, but it is an essential prospecting tool that provides you with the opportunity to display your small business finance expertise to thousands or even tens of thousands of prospects and sources of referral each and every month with the push of a button.

REVIEWS AND SERVICE COMPARISONS

There are dozens of quality email marketing companies for you to select from and one of the best ways to compare is to simply do an internet search for reviews of email marketing service providers. You'll find lots of comparisons and recommendations based on price and services. Most will have a "free look" period of up to 30 days where you can try the program at no cost. Another important consideration when making a final selection is your CRM. Many contact relationship managers have built-in integration with certain email service providers and such integration can save hours of work each month caused by duplicating contact entries.

Investing in a CRM System

NOTES

When it comes to software for your business, nothing will be more important (or necessary) than investing in a *Contact Relationship Manager* or CRM. In fact, if you are entering the industry with a career focus, you simply cannot operate without this essential prospecting and marketing management tool. CRMs are indispensable organizers for your lists and relationship building efforts.

A CRM is a software system, either located on your computer or cloud-based, in which you will store information about every aspect of your factoring broker business. It will manage your:

- ⇒ **CONTACT / RELATIONSHIP BUILDING PROCESSES**
- ⇒ **ACTIVITIES SCHEDULES**
- ⇒ **MARKETING CAMPAIGNS**
- ⇒ **PROSPECT LISTS**
- ⇒ **LENDERS DATABASE**

You will find you need a CRM from day one of operation and actually, even while you're learning the business. You will, for example, be visiting the websites of hundreds of factors and lenders, building a lenders database as you explore and categorizing each lender by its specialty areas of services. You will be building group lists of small business assistance organizations such as local SBDCs. (Small Business Development Centers). As you meet individuals from such organizations, you will create a record for each and begin the relationship building process.

YOU'LL NEED A CRM FROM DAY ONE

Established industry brokers with 3 or more years in the industry, can easily have thousands of prospects and sources of referral recorded in their CRM. Some truly seasoned brokers with over 10 years experience can have over 10,000 contacts. There is simply no way to organize such numbers effectively unless you do so electronically. A first task as you set up your office and factoring broker operation is to research and purchase a quality CRM.

Flyers and Brochures

You'll will find an almost immediate need for a quality brochure and probably several flyers when you begin your marketing efforts as a broker. If you have a little design experience and software such as Adobe's *InDesign* or *Microsoft Publisher*, a quality 3-panel brochure is not very difficult to create.

free!

Request Our FREE Booklet..."*When Banks Say NO!!..The Small Business Guide to Factoring*" from our website or contact us directly by phone.

Can't Say Yes to That Lucrative Contract?

With the economy in full recession and bank credit more difficult to obtain than ever, obtaining working capital for a small business can be a daunting task. And, good contracts and opportunities are scarce. Often, a great contract or job opportunity means 45 day, 60 day, 75day or even longer payment terms. This means that you will have to carry your "exploding" payroll while waiting for that first check to finally come in.

For many startups and young companies with a limited cash on hand, such contracts seem to be simply out of reach. But that is often not the case. Establishing an **Accounts Receivable Factoring** arrangement for your business can:

- **Provide weekly advances against invoices so you can make payroll**
- **Help you meet 941 tax payments**
- **Give you working capital to pay suppliers on time (and take discounts)**
- **Allow you to seek out contracts with those creditworthy but slow paying large customers you have avoided for years**

Factoring is the financing mechanism of choice for many small businesses in today's challenging economy and you can find out more by visiting our website and requesting our FREE Booklet... ***When Banks Say NO!...The Small Business Guide to Factoring.***

If you don't have any design experience, you can create inexpensive brochures using pre-printed brochure stock from companies like *PaperDirect* (www.paperdirect.com), *StockLayouts* (www.stocklayouts.com) and many others. With such companies, you'll simply order pre-printed, nicely designed brochure stock and then fill in the blanks using your computer and word processor.

When you begin marketing in earnest, you will find uses for dozens of specialized flyers and brochures which target specific groups or industries. For example, you may have a unique brochure for service companies or may take it even one step further and have a specific brochure for staffing companies, maintenance companies, guards services, and many others. Brochures and flyers are strong marketing tools and you will need at least one tri-fold or bi-fold brochure from day one.

DRIVE VISITORS TO YOUR WEBSITE

Brochures and flyers are also great tools for driving visitors to your website and will help immensely with your list building and email marketing efforts. Make sure your brochure contains a quality call-to-action free offer such as a booklet on factoring, factoring case study, or similar white paper. Have your contact information located in a panel on the back of the brochure and make certain your web address is printed on the brochure at least two times.

HAVE A GREAT PROBLEM HEADLINE

To draw attention to your brochures and flyers, always have a great "problem" headline that a business owner can understand. Get the reader's attention and then present the solution to the problem (factoring) on the inside panels. Brochures are a visual sales tool so use lots of meaningful and colorful graphics along with your copy.

Envelopes, Reply Envelopes, & Letterhead

NOTES

When it comes to marketing, envelopes, stuffers, brochures will all be very special in design. You will, however, need some very basic office supplies for everyday communications. This will include:

- **ENVELOPES:** Plain white envelopes (#10) imprinted with your business return address. No more than a hundred.
- **REPLY ENVELOPES:** Plain white envelopes (#9) imprinted with your return address. No more than a hundred.
- **LETTERHEAD:** A decent quality letterhead with all of your contact information (including web domain). This can usually be printed as needed if you have *Microsoft Word* or a similar word processing product .

Your goal here is simply to give a professional appearance on the rare occasion a regular letter is needed without breaking the bank. You will be surprised at just how little of this stock you'll really use in today's electronic world.

Additional Essential Software

ALMOST REQUIRED SOFTWARE

Microsoft Office software is almost required for those seriously in the business of consulting. There are several different *Office* packages available but you will certainly find you need both *Microsoft Word (or Publisher)* and *PowerPoint.* You will find you need *Word / Publisher* for documents such as brochures, flyers, case studies, workshop handouts, etc. You will need *PowerPoint* for your workshop slide presentations. In addition, you will also need to be able to open *Word* documents (such as your Broker's Agreements) that are sent to you via email in *Word* format.

CLOUD VERSIONS

If this suite of programs was not installed on your computer when you purchased it or you did not upgrade to it at a later date, *Microsoft* now offers an annual cloud subscription version which can be downloaded for considerably less than purchasing the entire *Office* suite. If you have a laptop you intend to use for workshop presentations but also have a desktop for your office, you will need a subscription that allows at least two downloads since you will want *PowerPoint* installed on both systems.

Take a "Soft Skills" Inventory

SELDOM COME NATURALLY

Very few (if any) individuals entering the business development side of the factoring /asset-based finance industry, are prepared to do so from day one. Real success as a factoring broker requires a unique combination of both hard and soft skills which seldom appear naturally, nor can they be found in a description of any college major or similar concentration of studies.

That's probably good news for industry "newbies", since most entering the broker community will have no significant advantage over others. For example, university graduates majoring in finance and even MBAs will have little real knowledge of factoring. And the very few that may have some knowledge of the inner workings of factoring and other business finance alternatives will likely have developed none of the "soft skills" necessary to succeed on the business development side. <u>In almost every case, such skills will need to be developed by you over time</u>.

MUST BE DEVELOPED OVER TIME

There are dozens of skillsets and personal traits which are defined as soft skills. But for those launching a business as a freelance factoring broker, there are several of really premier importance where you will need to focus some attention. These are:

LEARN TO SPEAK FLUENTLY

- **PERSONAL SPEAKING SKILLS:** You must have a good command of the English language and there really are NO exceptions here. You should both speak and write fluently. If you need to upgrade your speaking skills, start doing so immediately and there are hundreds of free or inexpensive methods available <u>There is no way to project the professional image required in this business and build the right kind of relationships necessary if you cannot speak fluently and write skillfully</u>.
- **PRESENTATION SKILLS:** Developing your small audience presentation skills will add thousands to your income each and every year. You will probably find as you develop your language skills, your presentation skills will improve right along with them.

- **SELF CONFIDENCE:** This is another personal trait and necessity which will probably improve substantially as you improve your speaking and communications skills. From a purely "hard skill" product knowledge standpoint, passing the broker *Proficiency Exam* at IACFB will go a long way in providing you with the self confidence you will need to project your expert status when networking with local professionals.

PERSISTENCE AND PERSEVERANCE

- **PERSISTENCE & PERSEVERANCE:** Those that can overcome challenges and deal with obstacles will find a much easier path to success. This is especially true when you are first starting out. The exceptional income potential which accompanies successful entry into this industry is waiting for those self-starters that have determination and can stick with it.

- **NETWORKING / RELATIONSHIP BUILDING SKILLS:** The ability to be both interesting and interested at the same time in conversations is important. Building relationships based on an "expert status" in your field will go a long way in creating the fertile ground required for developing profitable referral networks.

  THE 800 POUND GORILLA IN THE ROOM

  As you will learn in the following chapter on marketing, face-to-face networking is the 800 pound gorilla in the room. In fact, if you can become a talented networker and successfully build relationships with professionals you meet in banking, accounting, and law, and can combine that with perseverance, it will only be a matter of time until your business succeeds and succeeds in a big way.

- **WRITING SKILLS:** Solid writing skills are one of the more difficult soft skills to develop. If you are one of the many chattering away on social media, you are probably losing your grammatical competence faster than it can be replaced. When it comes to networking, being "published" will help significantly in establishing credentials. If you lack good writing skills, look into taking a local college course or two to help develop them. They will assist you in establishing your expert status.

Is It Time for a Personal Tune Up?

A career as a consultant in factoring and commercial finance means you will be engaging with all types of individuals and many on a very professional level. As we said, having good communication skills is essential. But just as important is how people perceive you when you walk into a room. Do you project the image of a true professional? If not, you may need a "personal tune-up".

ONE CHANCE TO MAKE A FIRST IMPRESSION

As it is always said, *you only have one chance to make a first impression.* And you will find that making a good first impression will make the processes of networking and relationship building just that much easier. We're not talking about hiring a professional image consultant here. But spicing up a wardrobe, changing a hairdo, or shedding a few extra pounds can often work wonders for your confidence when entering new and unfamiliar territory.

BETTER TO BE OVER DRESSED

- **UPGRADE YOUR APPAREL:** Financial consulting tends to be a suit and tie business. You will be networking with professionals such as bankers, accountants, and attorneys. As a whole, this is not a casually dressed group. When attending your first meetings and events frequented by such professionals, it will always be better to be a little overdressed rather than underdressed.
- **GROOMING:** From time to time, almost everyone tends to get a little lax regarding their grooming. Take a little time to take personal stock and make improvements as needed.
- **HIT THE GYM:** There are too many benefits to mention here regarding exercise. Its positive effects on productivity are well known and for many people, shedding a few extra pounds can greatly improve your business appearance. If you already belong to a gym, use it. If not, become a member of a large one. Exercise facilities can offer exceptional networking and relationship building opportunities as a membership bi-product since you will already have something in common with everyone you meet.

- **TRANSPORTATION:** As shallow as it may sound, you will be judged by what you drive to appointments, meetings, and events. It is also unavoidable that there will be occasions where you will be the designated driver, transporting those you are trying to impress.

  You will probably have need for occasional four passenger seating. No matter how you are dressed or groomed, if you pull up to a meeting in a dented or rusty vehicle with rips in the seat cushions and smoke coming out of the tailpipe, you're doomed. So, the rule here is don't go crazy, but upgrade if necessary. You certainly don't need the latest version of an expensive German import, but your vehicle needs to be clean and free of visual signs of age and neglect. The right vehicle will greatly enhance your image as a successful industry consultant so don't make the wrong personal impression with what you drive. Think very conservatively, however!

UPGRADE IF NECESSARY

The Bottom Line

In any business involving sales, having a high level of self esteem is vitally important to success. In short, you just really need to feel good about yourself and your appearance to be effective. If there are some personal characteristics about yourself which you feel need some attention, start to address them now. Get help and advice from those you trust. There are also thousands of excellent books and publications available to help you along in this important area.

The great news here is this. There is very little about a person's personal appearance or lack of particular soft skills that cannot be addressed and remedied. For many, a successful entry into the business development side of the factoring and small business finance industry can represent an incredible opportunity for a total lifestyle makeover. This is a career path you should look at as much more than a simple business opportunity. You can make your entry into this extraordinary industry a lifestyle "happening".

LITTLE THAT CANNOT BE ADDRESSED

Pre-Opening Planning & Research

Before you begin your first marketing and networking efforts, you'll need to do some planning and research in five specific areas.

- **CLUBS & ORGANIZATIONS:** Because networking and relationship building are so vitally important to your business, you will need to begin researching local organizations which will be the best for you to join.
- **LENDERS DATABASE:** You cannot refer business until you know where to refer it. This will be an ongoing task but now is the time to begin building your lenders database.

JOINING SOCIAL MEDIA

- **SOCIAL MEDIA:** If you do not already have them, set up both a *LinkedIn* and *Facebook* account. You will probably utilize both.
- **MEASURING YOUR KNOWLEDGE:** Take the Proficiency Exam and measure your knowledge. Know your stuff before you begin attending networking events. You will be answering questions and explaining your business. There is a direct link to the exam at the IACFB's Learning Lab at the Brokers Forum. This exam is not about passing. It is about being an **expert**. Make certain you can score a 90% or higher on the IACFB broker Proficiency Exam before embarking. Take it as many times as necessary.

BUSINESS LICENSING

- **LICENSING, BONDING & INSURANCE:** You will need to get your business legal and this includes applying for your local business license. If you are operating in California, there's unfortunately more.

Joining Clubs and Organizations

Becoming an active member of local clubs and organizations will play a big role in your networking and relationship building efforts. In most communities of size, you will have dozens of great clubs and organizations to choose from so you need to do a little research before you make any decisions. For most factoring brokers, it is likely you will join at least two or three organizations over time.

Bear in mind that networking and relationship building is not simple. To be a successful networker involves a lot of commitment and hard work. Joining clubs and organizations is not like subscribing to a magazine you can read once and pitch. So the rule here is, unlike magazines, don't oversubscribe. It is much better to join just one or two clubs and organizations and devote serious time to them, rather joining a dozen groups where you never succeed in building real relationships due to the limited time you spend with each.

DON'T OVERSUBSCRIBE

To get the most from joining clubs and organizations, make sure you join those you have a genuine interest in. In each organization you select, you want to eventually become one of the club's movers and shakers. You don't just want to serve on committees, you want to run committees. Work your way up to being a true organizer within the group. This is where you will get the greatest benefit and most attention. Before you join any organization, however, we will AGAIN give you very strong word of caution. KNOW YOUR STUFF!

You will always be in reputation-building mode as you interact with others. Make certain you are very comfortable with your level of factoring knowledge. Prepare to often be the center of attention as those you meet strive to learn more about you and what you do.

What to Join

When it comes to joining networking organizations, you will have dozens or even hundreds of choices depending on the size of your city. Here are a few of the most popular choices for factoring brokers.

- **CHAMBER OF COMMERCE:** This is basically an essential for all factoring brokers. Your local *Chamber* will be overflowing with bank lending officers, accountants, attorneys, and small business owners.
  Cost to Join: On average $300 - $400 per year.
- **TOASTMASTERS:** If your public speaking skills and grammar need some attention, here is where to go. There are well over 15,000 active *Toastmaster* clubs worldwide but not all *Toastmasters* are the same. Each club is unique. Visit several and find the club just right one for you.
  Cost to Join: On average $75 - $100 per year.

JOIN YOUR LOCAL CHAMBER OF COMMERCE AND TOASTMASTERS

- **COMMUNITY SERVICE ORGANIZATIONS:** Joining a community service organization not only helps you connect with the movers and shakers in your community, it also helps you become one. The benefits of getting involved in community service and volunteerism by joining clubs and organization such as *Rotary, Lions, Elks,* or *Kiwanis* are too numerous to mention, but almost all who join such organizations find the experience personally satisfying and rewarding. These clubs expect their members to do business with each other and most allow only one member from each type of profession. **Cost to Join:** On average $100 - $400 per year.

COMMUNITY AND CHARITABLE ORGANIZATIONS

- **OTHER COMMUNITY / CHARITABLE ORGANIZATIONS:** Getting involved with a local charity or two should be high on your list when it comes to meeting influential people in your community. Such organizations can be church related or non-profits such as food banks, shelters for the homeless, soup kitchens, etc. They can be geared to a specific demographic like *Junior Leagues International,* which focuses on women and their role in civic leadership within the community or organizations like *Habitat for Humanity* with its focus on affordable housing for low income families. **Cost to Join:** Free - $500

CLUBS THAT ARE ALL ABOUT YOU

- **PERSONAL INTEREST CLUBS:** This is a very broad category and can include everything from local car clubs to gardening clubs. Like to fish from a kayak? Join a kayaking club. Into model railroading? There's probably a club for that right in your area. Do some research and get involved in something you're passionate about. Joining a personal interest club or group may provide networking opportunities, but its also all about you.

Measure Your Working Knowledge

Before you open your doors for business and begin your day-to-day routine of prospecting for leads and referrals, you need to make certain of your industry knowledge. You will not become the expert you need to be overnight. In fact, it will probably take several months of hard work and research before you reach the level of knowledge you really need to attain.

CREDENTIALED PROFESSIONALS

One of the greatest fears of all new industry brokers first entering the industry is that they will be exposed as a neophyte at networking events. They are terrified to get into conversations with certain "credentialed" professionals such as CPAs and bankers about business finance because of a their perceived lack of knowledge.

PROFICIENCY EXAM

As previously mentioned, to help you overcome this, we have prepared a "Proficiency Exam" to help you measure your level of knowledge. The exam is provide by IACFB and can be accessed by visiting the *Learning Lab* at the Factoring 101 Broker Forums. After you have registered and been set up with *Learning Lab* permissions, you will have access to the exam. The test is 200 questions which are taken from a databank of over 450 questions and is based on information contained solely in this guide. (see page 195)

Licensing, Bonding and Insurance

BROKER LICENSING

Before you begin operations, you will naturally need to "get legal" and this includes obtaining a local business license. There is also the matter of insurance, typically in the form of professional liability insurance or errors & omissions insurance to cover you in the event you are named as a party to a lawsuit involving a finance company you recommended. Unfortunately, we live in a very litigious world and its best to be on the safe side. Speak with your insurance agent.

In the state of California, brokers involved with commercial lending are required to obtain a *California Finance Lenders License*, even though you have no contracting responsibilities in the loan process. While there is no testing mandated at this time, you are required to have a minimum net worth of $25,000, post a $25,000 surety bond, and not have a criminal history.

BUSINESS DEVELOPMENT STRATEGIES

Learning to Market & Network

Now that you have a better understanding of your product and services, its time to talk about business development or in more direct terms, how you earn money as an independent industry broker. But before we get started, you need to understand a few marketing concepts so you will have a better feel for creating a marketing plan that works for your business.

It's All About Lead Generation

FOCUS WILL ALWAYS BE LEAD GENERATION

Each and every day, your goal as an industry broker will focus on something called *lead generation*. It could not be more simple. The various marketing tools an individual broker may choose to utilize in order to generate such leads will vary from person to person, depending on their particular circumstances. Some career factoring brokers will market intensively. Others, operating on what can be described as an "occasional basis", will barely market at all. Either way, no matter what group you fit into, your focus will be exactly the same. You will simply be engaged in generating leads.

As a factoring broker, you will never become involved in tedious paperwork. You have absolutely no business responsibilities when it comes to:

NO RESPONSIBILITIES

- **Contracting with a client**
- **Filing security agreements**
- **Performing background checks**
- **Doing credit analysis**
- **Funding**

In fact, its unlikely you will ever actually be the person that closes a deal. Your normal business day will typically focus on completing just three (3) tasks.

- **Generating quality leads for factoring / business financing services**
- **Qualifying those leads**
- **Submitting your qualified leads to a lender**

ITS ALL ABOUT LEAD GENERATION

Since some percentage of your leads will become qualified leads and some percentage of your qualified leads will become factoring clients, it should be crystal clear the more leads you generate, the more clients you will generate and the faster your business and income will grow. So again, your business is very, very simple. Its all about lead generation. And to generate those leads, you will use marketing.

Marketing Defined

Marketing terminology is a bit dynamic with new definitions and phrases being coined almost daily. The rapid growth of the internet and social media has been the catalyst for all types of new marketing creations and strategies. They are everywhere and it seems new books are being written daily by "new age" marketing gurus who tout their sure fire method for making a million using the internet and "their system". And, they all seem to have a new definition of for our old friend, marketing.

For our purposes, however, we are going to define marketing as something quite simple. Marketing will be:

"anything you do to promote your business"

The ultimate goal of marketing for your consultancy is to present or communicate the value of your financial services to small business owners in need of them. This will very often involve education. In fact, a great number of the marketing methods you will employ for business development will focus heavily on educating small business owners about the availability of this thing called factoring and a few other financing alternatives to traditional bank loans.

Primary Marketing Styles

HOW DO I GENERATE LEADS?

Since the business of brokering is all about lead generation and you know you need to market to do that, the obvious question then becomes: *How do I do that? What marketing methods do I use to generate these leads?*

The answer is you will use two primary marketing types or styles. These are *inbound marketing* and *outbound marketing.* And the reality is this. When it comes to generating new commission-generating leads and clients for factoring brokers, both inbound marketing and outbound marketing work pretty well. In fact, recent factoring industry polls continue to reflect the fact that when it comes to bringing in new clients for factoring, its about a 50/50 split. Roughly one half of all new clients are the result of some inbound marketing strategy and the other half come from some form of outbound marketing.

ITS A 50 / 50 SPLIT

Which of these methods is right for you and which you choose to primarily focus on will be determined by your marketing budget and whether you are attacking this industry with a career motivation or you are simply looking for a little extra part-time income. In either case, both seem to do the job just fine if you can become accomplished in their use.

Outbound Marketing

CALL-TO-ACTION
INTERRUPTION
MARKETING

Outbound marketing revolves around *direct marketing* or its more favored modern name, *direct response marketing.* This is because all direct marketing messages are designed to induce an immediate response or a call-to-action from the receiver of the message. The response can be to return a reply card, a request to call, or to click the link to a website, etc. Direct response marketing is also sometimes termed *interruption marketing* because it interrupts the receiver with a coercive message to act right now.

Outbound marketing utilizes many methods to deliver its powerful call-to-action message. These include *direct mail, classified ads, cold calling, canvassing, email marketing, television advertising, radio advertising, holding workshops*, etc. No matter what the delivery method used, however, the message is always the same:

ACT RIGHT NOW...BEFORE ITS TOO LATE!

INBOUND
PERMISSIONS
MARKETING

Inbound Marketing

In modern marketing circles, *inbound marketing* is all the rage. Marketing gurus simply can't talk enough about it. Using the various strategies common to inbound marketing (sometimes referred to as *permission marketing*), you will promote your business utilizing *social media, blogs, e-newsletters, podcasts, featured guest public speaking, press releases, word of mouth, networking, authoring*, etc.

INBOUND
MARKETING
STRATEGY

STRATEGY VISITORS LEADS CUSTOMERS PROMOTERS

Inbound marketing is a term coined by *Brian Halligen*, CEO and co-founder of the internet marketing company, *HubSpot.* As opposed to outbound direct response marketing, inbound marketing revolves around marketing activities that attract prospective customers to a website, social media hub, or blogspot by producing interesting and informative articles and content. Strategies common to inbound marketing also tend to be the cornerstones in the relationship building process, a primary goal for all those with a focus on building solid referral networks.

What's Right for You?

NOTES

The probability is, most factoring brokers will use some combination of inbound and outbound marketing as they start out. What tools they use will often be determined by how proficient or skilled they are at employing a particular market method. Almost all will want to try some direct mail since everyone comes equipped with the means to stuff an envelope and apply a stamp. Others will want to dive into social media since they are already engulfed in it anyway and know how to tweet and post on an expert level.

SOCIAL MEDIA WILL FAIL MISERABLY

Unfortunately, when utilized as "top billing", these two tools will return almost zero results when it comes to your factoring consultancy. They will fail and fail miserably. They can, however, be very beneficial when used in a supporting role. For example, direct mail can garner very good response when used to announce a workshop or to alert a group of business owners about a free report or case study available on your website.

Marketing: Success or Failure

So your success in the industry will all come down to marketing. In fact, if you excel in marketing as a factoring consultant, the rest of the business really takes care of itself. While you may have thought the work involved to become a broker was acquiring an in-depth knowledge of the products, you were wrong. True, you must have the knowledge. But factoring and its related CORE areas of finance are really very simple in structure and anyone can learn everything they need to know in a short time and certainly within a few weeks.

THE "WORK" IS TO DEVELOP YOUR MARKETING SKILLS

The work, and what separates success from failure in the industry, is marketing. It is not likely, as you start out, that you have the all the necessary marketing skills you need to truly succeed. What tends to separate successful brokers from industry dropouts is their drive to develop and acquire the marketing skills necessary to generate the quality leads (in sufficient numbers) to earn the commission income that has made the factoring industry famous.

Defining Your Business Goals

SET REALISTIC BUSINESS GOALS

You need to have some business goals in mind when you begin operations. For some, this will be a relatively easy task. You may simply say, "*I want to be at the $100,000 + income level within three years.*" Well, that's certainly a goal and it is probably very attainable. But it's a little too simplistic. Setting realistic business goals actually involves a little bit more thought and this is especially true for freelancers. As a factoring broker, you need to keep focused and make your goals very specific. Try not to drift!

There are many sites you can visit on the web with good references and interesting articles for setting business goals. One can be found at *The Goal Setting Guide* (www.goal-setting-guide.com) which utilizes a model called "SMART" goal setting. The SMART model is easy to understand and one which most should be able to adhere to. Business goals using this model should be:

THE "SMART" MODEL

- **SPECIFIC:** Specific relates to What, Why, and How of the SMART model. Examples of your goals might be:

  - **What**: *I'm going to build a factoring broker business which generates $10,000 + in monthly income.*

  - **Why**: *My company is downsizing and I fear losing my job.*

  - **How**: *I'm going to build an extensive network of referral sources.*

- **MEASURABLE:** Your goal should be easily measurable: For example: *I'm going to add at least one new client every month.*

MAKE YOUR GOALS ATTAINABLE

- **ATTAINABLE:** Don't set your goals out of reach. For example, the previous goal of *adding one new client at least per month* is very attainable.
- **REALISTIC**: Do you have the skillsets and abilities to achieve your goal? For example, if your goal is to: *Bring in 2 new clients per month using a monthly workshop program.* Do you have the necessary skill (public speaking) to do so?
- **TIMELY:** Set a reachable timeframe for your goal such as 6 months, 12 months 2 years, etc. Set an endpoint for your goal.

Reaching the $100,000 Mark

NOTES

Reaching the $100,000 income level tends to be a "rite of passage" for most industry brokers and that is understandable. You are a freelance professional consultant, and that is a consultant's wage. What will it take for you to reach that goal? From the numbers side, surprisingly little. From the work side, quite a lot. Here is the numbers side.

RITE OF PASSAGE

STOCKBROKERS: We have all met stockbrokers. They are financial consultants too. They primarily deal with consumers. In today's marketplace, in order to take home $100,000 per year, a stockbroker will need between $75,000,000 and $125,000,000 under his or her management. That's $75-$125 million dollars. A stockbroker will need to get "x" number of clients to WRITE checks for millions and millions of dollars. But it is a great business, requiring a great deal of knowledge, and most successful stockbrokers reach that level of earnings and even more.

FACTORING BROKERS: Factoring brokers are a bit different. They deal with business owners. In today's marketplace, in order to earn the same $100,000 per year, a factoring broker will only need $2,000,000 to $3,000,000 under management. That's just $2-$3 million dollars. Of greater importance, the money goes the other way. Clients RECEIVE checks from factors, not WRITE checks to them.

JUST $2,000,000. How do we calculate just $2,000,000? Very easy!

Let's say a factoring broker has developed 20 clients over the course of 2 years. Less than one per month. Each client is of small to average size (print shops, janitorial services, small manufacturers, etc.) and let's say each factors just $100,000 in invoices each month or $2,000,000 total (20 x $100,000).

LESS THAN ONE AVERAGE CLIENT PER MONTH

At an average factoring discount of just 3%, that will generate a total of $60,000 per month in total fees. As the broker of record, you will receive between 10-15 percent of those fees. Let's use a 12.5% average which will give us an income of $7,500 per month or $90,000 per year. That assumes all invoices are paid at 30 days. Longer payment times will increase fees as well as your income.

Developing Your Marketing Plan

You will need to develop a marketing plan. It does not have to be elaborate, but you need a plan. You will find tens of thousands of articles on the web regarding how to develop a good marketing plan and they will all impart some great tips. But you are a consultant in a very specialized field and your marketing strategies will differ significantly, from say, a florist or a auto repair shop owner.

In his classic book, *Ogilvie on Advertising*, David Ogilvy addresses the challenges of advertising and these dovetail perfectly with what you, as a factoring broker, will face. Challenges like...

* *I don't know who you are*
* *I don know your company*
* *I don't know your company's product*
* *I don't know what your company stands for*
* *I don't know your company's record*
* *I don't know your company's reputation*
* *Now...what was it you wanted to sell me?*

So when developing your marketing plan, a great place to start would be to focus on addressing the statements above. They provide a perfect road map to building a marketing plan for your consultancy. To address these challenges, you may use dozens of different marketing tools. But with every campaign you create, you should be addressing one or more of the challenges above. The more overlap a campaign has, the better. Some marketing tools will be limited on their impact. A simple business card, for example, will address the first three challenges. A well designed website can easily address all seven.

A major component of your business is one of education. Most small business owners know little of factoring or the other products you represent. But not only do you need to educate, you need to develop, combine, and format the types of marketing strategies which will allow you to both educate and at the same time, position yourself as THE "expert" consultant that can get the job done.

About Your Marketing Budget

When it comes to developing a marketing budget, factoring brokers are very fortunate. This is due to the fact that networking, and especially face-to-face networking, can be such a productive tool for business development. As opposed to direct marketing, networking tends to be very inexpensive. No matter what your initial monetary limitations are, when it comes to marketing your business, you can almost always find a myriad of affordable networking opportunities available in your own community or within a short drive.

INEXPENSIVE NETWORKING OPPORTUNITIES

Marketing Cost / Benefit Analysis

You really cannot create a realistic marketing budget for your consultancy without at least sketching out a rough analysis of costs vs. benefits and here's the reason. The referral commissions (benefits) paid to independent brokers in the factoring industry are so generous, that almost any marketing expense (cost) to generate a client can be easily justified.

If you calculate the monthly commission on even a relatively small account of say $50,000 in invoice purchases per month, you'll find you will earn somewhere between $250 and $350 monthly. That's $3,000 to over $4,000 per year. And we know that once contracted, it is not unusual for a business to employ the services of its factor for 3,4, even 5 years or longer. That means the broker of record will earn a whopping $9,000 to $20,000 on that single account over its life. There are no maintenance costs or additional service expenses paid by the broker. Once the client is referred, all the broker will do is open a welcome envelope every month containing a commission check.

So what is the other side of the equation? What is the marketing cost to generate that one account? Maybe it was just a few hundred dollars in classified ads. Maybe it was $500 paid for some radio spots. Maybe it was $1,000 paid for a sponsorship. It really makes little difference. A cost / benefit analysis, when applied to the costs of marketing vs. commissions generated for factoring brokers, is so skewed towards the latter, as to make the discussion almost always inconsequential.

EXCEPTIONAL COST / BENEFIT COMPARISON

Marketing...What Works

Since you are about to spend a good portion of your time focused on generating quality factoring leads, its probably a good idea to learn what types of marketing tend to work better than others for our industry so you can avoid the time wasters. Here's what we know works for our industry.

TAKES TIME TO REAP BENEFITS

⇒ **FACE-TO-FACE NETWORKING:** This is the 800 pound gorilla in the room. The downside is it takes time to reap the benefits. But if you build meaningful relationships with bank loan officers, accounting professionals, and members of business support groups (S.C.O.R.E., SBDCs, EDCs, etc.), business will certainly come your way.

⇒ **WORKSHOPS:** Your most important direct marketing tool, workshops can be utilized as soon as you have compiled a quality prospect list. Though it may take six months or longer from the time you open your doors until you can give your first workshop, this single tool, along with a little public speaking, can keep your sales pipeline full of prospects.

⇒ **DIRECT MAIL:** Use only in conjunction with a newsletter or an event (workshop, promotion, disaster) and only if followed up with a phone call. You will likely be very disappointed with "mass" mailing results. The structure of your mail message should always give you a reason (excuse) to follow up with a phone call to the prospect.

A VERY POTENT WEAPON

⇒ **CREATIVE SPONSORSHIPS:** For networking, creative sponsorships can be a very, very, potent weapons. (see the *Bankers Bash page 177)*

⇒ **NEWSLETTERS & ARTICLE WRITING:** Newsletters (in print format) can generate excellent leads on a local basis. Writing articles for local publication as well as online is a powerful tool and "credentials builder" when it comes to compiling an expert reputation.

⇒ **CLASSIFIED ADS:** Use these in publications where you see the owners of service sector businesses advertising their companies. Classified ads are inexpensive, a good place to start, and can lead to some very pleasant surprises.

Your Primary Target Groups

Your targets for marketing can be categorized into two very broad MAIN segments or groups.

1. **PROSPECTS GROUP:** A demographic target group of small B2B business owners who may need the services of a factor now or in the future.
2. **REFERRAL GROUP:** A target group made up of local community professionals who through referral, can send business your way.

Roughly 50% of all new factoring clients are sourced using some form of direct response marketing. The source of these new factoring clients will be your PROSPECTS GROUPS.

Roughly 50% of all new factoring clients are sourced as a result of referral from a professional such as an accountant, banker, etc. This would be the result of networking with members of your REFERRALS GROUPS.

SUBDIVIDING PROSPECT GROUPS

Members of your first target group, your PROSPECTS GROUP, can be subdivided many ways. You may subdivide the list into sectors:

- **SERVICE SECTOR**
- **MANUFACTURING / DISTRIBUTION SECTOR**
- **GOVERNEMNT CONTRACTORS SECTOR**
- **CONSTRUCTION RELATED SECTOR**
- **RETAIL COMPANIES SECTOR**

DIVIDING INTO SUB-SECTORS

You can further subdivide your sectors into sub-sectors. You can, for example, subdivide your SERVICE SECTOR CATEGORY into:

- **Guard Services**
- **Staffing Companies**
- **Landscaping Companies**
- **Janitorial Services**
- **Maintenance Companies**
- **Freight Companies**

Members of your second target group, your REFERRAL GROUP, can also be subdivided dozens of ways. For example, you may create sub-groups of:

- **BUSINESS SUPPORT / INCUBATOR STAFF**
- **ACCOUNTING PROFESSIONALS**
- **LENDING OFFICERS**
- **BANKING PROFESSIONALS**
- **ATTORNEYS**
- **INSURANCE PROFESSIONALS (COMMERCIAL)**
- **BUSINESS BROKERS**

You can further subdivide these sub-groups into more manageable lists. You can subdivide your BUSINESS SUPPORT / INCUBATORS into:

- **SCORE members**
- **SBDC members (Small Business Development Centers)**
- **EDC members (Economic Development Centers)**
- **BAC members (Business Assistance Centers)**
- **Other Local Business Incubators**

SEASONED BROKERS MAY HAVE 7,500 CONTACTS OR MORE

As you know, it is not unusual for a seasoned industry factoring broker (one who has been in the industry 3 or more years) to have 2,500, 5,000, 7,500 or even more individuals in their various groups.

To market to such numbers efficiently, you must subdivide and manage each group. For example, if you stumble across an interesting online article on how factoring benefitted a small service sector business, you would probably want to send a targeted email with a link to that article to your service sector companies only. If you found an article on how a bookkeeper had doubled her client base by helping them source business loans, you would certainly want to send a link to that article to your accounting group. To do so, you will need the help of some quality contact relationship management software (CRM) and a good email marketing service.

The Importance of List Building

When you first launch your brokering business, a great deal of your marketing efforts will be focused on list building. In fact, you will always be adding to or pruning your various lists. List building is an essential part of marketing your business and you can't ignore it. There are four primary types of lists you will be dealing with:

- **DATABANK LISTS:** Databank lists are commercially available lists that you order and are purchased based upon demographics. For example, you might order a list of 300 manufacturers and distributors in 7 or 8 local zip codes around you. You will order the owner's name, the business address, and a phone number. These lists, purchased from list brokers, can be a great way to "prime the pump" and get things started when you first open your doors.

A GREAT WAY TO PRIME THE PUMP

- **COMPILED LISTS:** Compiled lists are those you personally construct from sources such as trade magazines, trade shows, internet research, members of professional associations, etc. Where databank lists are usually used for some form of direct mail solicitation, compiled lists may be employed for face-to-face marketing or telephone solicitation in conjunction with a workshop or luncheon seminar.

- **E-LISTS:** E-lists are used for email marketing and are a powerful tool for all factoring brokers. Unfortunately, they are also the most difficult and time consuming lists to produce. E-lists are made up of opt-ins from your website. They contain the names of website visitors requesting newsletters, additional information, a free report, etc. All members of your e-lists MUST be opt-in. You should avoid purchasing an e-list from a list broker.

NEVER PURCHASE AN E-LIST

- **RESPONSE LISTS:** Response lists are comprised of members of your databank, compiled, and e-lists that have <u>responded</u> to one of your offers. They have requested a free booklet, asked to attend a workshop, replied to a classified ad, or contacted you through your website. Response lists are your "PROSPECT" lists. Members of response lists are often just one phone call away from becoming a commission-generating client.

YOUR MOST VALUABLE LIST

Service Businesses That Employ Factoring

There are hundreds of types of businesses from the various business sectors that have been known to employ factoring. If purchasing a databank list or constructing a complied list, below is a short list of service related industries you may wish to focus on.

- Passenger / Bus Transportation
- Freight and Trucking
- Air Transportation
- Water Delivery
- Limousine Services
- Warehouse / Storage Facilities
- Broadcasting Services
- Internet Services
- Telecommunication Services
- Sound Recording Services
- Data Processing Services
- Property Management Services
- Equipment Rental Services
- Environmental Testing Services
- Accounting / Bookkeeping Services
- Engineering / Design Services
- Drafting Services
- Building Inspection Services
- Surveying Services
- Computer System Design
- Environmental Consulting
- Technical Consulting
- Advertising Services
- Marketing Research Companies
- Photographers
- Office Administration Services
- Staffing / Employment Services
- Telephone Call Centers
- Pest Control Companies
- Janitorial Services
- Guard / Protection Services
- Detective Agencies
- Carpet Cleaners
- Waste Management Companies
- Commercial Building Maintenance
- Welders
- Remediation Services
- Medical Labs
- Child Care
- Tutoring / Education Services
- Sports Promotors
- Charter Bus Services
- Food Catering Companies
- Automotive Repair / Bodywork
- Electronics Repair Services
- Parking Lot Maintenance
- Linens and Uniforms Cleaners
- Market Research Providers
- Specialized Design Services
- Air Conditioning Maintenance

Manufacturers & Distributors That Employ Factoring

Of course, factoring is not just employed by the service sector. There are many manufacturers and distributors that utilize the services of factors as well. Below is a very small list of examples.

- Forestry / Logging
- Fishing and Hunting Products
- Paper Goods
- Agricultural / Growers
- Oil and Gas Producers
- Oil and Gas Support Products
- Mining (Coal and Mineral)
- Fertilizer Producers
- Commercial Construction
- Highway Bridge Construction
- Food Manufacturers / Gourmet Prod.
- Textile / Garment Manufacturers
- Footwear Manufacturers / Distributors
- Lumber / Wood Products
- Chemical Products
- Rubber Products
- Plastics Manufacturers
- Pharmaceutical Manufacturers
- Paints and Coatings
- Soaps and Cleaners
- Glass Products
- Pottery Products
- Metal Fabricators
- Durable Goods
- Automotive Accessories
- Commercial Equipment
- Refrigeration Manufacturers
- Hardware and Plumbing Supplies
- Sporting Goods
- Toys
- Hobby Crafts
- Jewelry
- Petroleum Related Products
- Beer / Wine / Craft Brewers
- Farm Supplies
- Flowers and Nurseries
- Tobacco Products
- Paint Manufacturers
- Electronics Manufacturers
- Lawn Equipment and Supplies
- General Hardware
- Newspaper / Magazine Publishers
- Book Distributors
- Power Sports Equipment Manufacturers
- Boats / Boating Equipment
- Specialty Aircraft Equipment
- Bakeries

Firing Up Your Marketing Engine

The time has come to open your doors. You have developed a high level of factoring expertise and also a working knowledge of the other niche and CORE product areas. Now it's time to start exploring your sales tools. Here's what we recommend:

BEGIN FILLING YOUR WHITE BOARD

- Start slow and test the waters. Don't blow your marketing budget on your first ideas.
- Focus heavily (80% of your time) on list building utilizing networking opportunities. Learn to use your CRM.
- Start attending some local small business workshops. Visit local SBDC, EDC, and SCORE websites and sign up for their newsletters which will include times and dates of events.
- Join a local Chamber of Commerce and start attending after hours meet ups. Your local Chamber of Commerce is the "big leagues" when it comes to networking.
- Begin filling your *white board* with upcoming events (see page 157). One of your very early goals is to have ZERO empty weeks on the *white board.* Once you have one solid networking event scheduled for each week, then focus on filling in the blanks day by day. Book yourself solid.
- Start placing some inexpensive classified ads in local publications as well as online venues based on your research.
- Look for locations where you can leave your brochures. The local Chamber of Commerce main offices will likely be one, but there are many other locations available as well.
- Work on a quality article on small business finance. The same publications you are using for your classifieds may be a great place to publish your first articles. Most are always looking for free content. We recommend a subject like: "*How to Finance Your Service Business*". Naturally, feature factoring as a method of finance.
- Set up the "invitation page" of your website with a free offer and begin testing some highly targeted direct mail. Focus on service sector companies at first. Use the same article you just authored for your offer of a "FREE Report".

A Secret Tool of Networking Pros

New brokers entering the industry will test the waters with all types of marketing programs and ideas to see what works. Because of its very low cost, social media participation and face-to-face networking should naturally be very high on that list. In fact, a broker's normal daily routine should always include at least one hour of planned networking. And one of the best methods of making sure you stick to this routine is with a simple, dry-erase white board wall calendar.

Though having a dry-erase calendar take the place of a day planner might seem a bit old fashioned in today's world of high technology, it is really anything but. One of your early goals as an industry broker is to literally immerse yourself in networking opportunities.

Strategic Planning: Filling the Board

To get the most from network marketing, you need plan ahead...at least four months ahead. Now is the time to begin filling the board. You can't avoid some overlap of scheduled meetings but the best way to avoid conflicts and a networking "drought" is with this simple in-your-face tool.

AVOID NETWORKING DROUGHTS

Research possible opportunities for your future networking and start fitting them on the board. Start with "premier events" first. Premier events are those that do not occur frequently and those you definitely do not want to miss. For example, a small business symposium held once a year by a local SBDC or a class on government contract financing for entrepreneurs sponsored by the SBA would be the types of events that could provide a learning experience, excellent prospecting opportunities, as well as the ability to meet with some very good sources of business referral.

HAVE AS LITTLE WHITE SPACE AS POSSIBLE

Log your local Chamber of Commerce events. These are an easy referral path to your local banking community. Virtually all bank loan officers periodically attend Chamber events. Add in weekly meeting dates of social and civic organizations. Then throw in some time for unscheduled but soon to be booked lunch dates. Your goal here is to have as little unfilled white space as possible.

Email Newsletter Marketing

When it comes to email marketing, building and managing lists is just half the formula for success. The other half is creating interesting, attention-getting content. And here's where it gets a little tricky. How do you create e-newsletter content that:

- will interest a prospective small business client, get them to contact you, and at the same time...
- interest a referral source and assist in the relationship building process with that referral source?

CREATING MULTIPLE NEWSLETTERS

That's easy! Publish multiple e-newsletters. In fact, we know broker "marketeers" that publish 3 or more e-newsletters each month. E-newsletter marketing is their primary source of lead generation. E-newsletters help to build relationships with both prospective clients and sources of referral. But where do they get all their fascinating content to create great newsletters? That's easy too, the internet!

On the web, its easy to find thousands of articles, polls, and blogposts dealing with great topics for any business related newsletter. Subjects will include:

- **CASHFLOW PROBLEMS OF BUSINESS**
- **GOVERNMENT REGULATION**
- **TAXES**
- **LENDING AND ACCESS TO CAPITAL**
- **HEALTH CARE**
- **THE ECONOMY**
- **HOW TO GENERATE NEW SALES**

KNOW THE HOT BUTTONS

Knowing the "hot buttons" of your readers will go a long way in helping you create newsletters that are opened and read. E-newsletters should never, however, focus entirely on just problems. You need to have other attention-getting content that is of the "general interest" type.

There are thousands of very good articles on the internet as well as excellent books on the subject of how to write and publish great e-newsletters. If you have never published a business newsletter, invest some spare time in learning how its done. When setting your goals, make one to add a certain amount of new subscribers to your email lists each and every month. Make the target attainable, but focus on meeting those goals and building your lists. A goal of 50 to 100 new subscribers each month is probably reachable in your first "networking intensive" months as you join new clubs and organizations. Remember, however, all subscribers must be opt-in.

The Importance of Offers

OFFERS TRIGGER A CALL-TO-ACTION

Offers are by far the most important component of any marketing campaign and especially outbound campaigns. They are designed to trigger a response and a call-to-action from the reader. Offers can be as simple as an e-newsletter subscription or they can be for free reports, white papers, booklets, workshops etc. Classified ads, your website, any direct mail, cold calls, etc. always must feature an offer.

So, when publishing your newsletter, always make certain it contains an offer for a case study, free report, booklet, etc. on small business finance. To get the offer, readers should visit a specific page on your website. That page should include two types of offers.

THE MOST COMMON OF ALL OFFERS

1. **SOFT OFFER:** This is the most common type of offer. It is "painless" from the receiver's point of view. It gives them the opportunity to say, *I may be interested. Tell me more.* Soft offers for factoring brokers will include reports, booklets, white papers on factoring, workshop invitations, etc.

2. **HARD OFFERS:** Hard offers involve personal contact in the form of a face-to-face meeting or a telephone call. Hard offers appeal to "serious" prospects ready to make a decision. For brokers, a typical hard offer would be: "*To speak with an underwriter about ready financing for your small business, just give us a call during normal business hours*".

More On Offers

Direct marketing, and even successful networking, is all about offers. Offers are the prime method used to build your business. In fact, absolutely nothing happens in business without an offer. An offer is *quid pro quo.* You do this for me and I'll do that for you. You sign up on my website and I'll give you my free report.

AN OFFER IS *QUID PRO QUO*

There are always two simple components to any offer. They are:

1. **What does the prospect get?**
2. **What does the prospect have to do to get it?**

In factoring, the offer is simple.

1. **What does the prospect get? Money on a timely basis to speed up problems of cash flow.**
2. **What does the prospect have to do to get it? Pay a factoring fee.**

To some, networking is really a form of advertising. It creates an awareness of your personal brand and your status as an expert in your field. There is no *quid pro quo* because you are not soliciting a sale. But the referral side of networking is different and based on a *quid pro quo* offer.

1. **What does your new referral source get? Referrals from you.**
2. **What does the referral source need to do to get it? Send some referrals back your way.**

Offers: Your Business Starting Point

BUSINESS DOES NOT HAPPEN WITHOUT AN OFFER

Now you understand business simply does not happen without offers and a level of acceptance to those offers. So to begin your marketing efforts, you need to create some basic offers. Every marketing event you launch MUST contain one or more offers.

Getting Leads Using Classified Ads

Classified advertising is a great marketing method to utilize when your just starting out and testing the waters. Classifieds are:

- **Inexpensive. This is one of the greatest advantages to utilizing classifieds.**
- **Used in conjunction with your website to provide an immediate and measurable response.**
- **Exceptional tools to help build your email lists through the use of offers.**
- **Able to generate an immediate "hard offer" contact response and prospective new client.**

SELECTING THE RIGHT PUBLICATION IS THE SECRET

When you place classified advertisements, you will normally be able to contract for multiple insertions and receive a discount. Many experts on classified advertising say a prospect needs to see your ad at least three times before they act. Others say up to seven. Either way, when you select a publication to place your ads, plan on multiple insertions over a period of at least four to six weeks.

Use small classified ads that focus on problems of PAYROLL to generate service company leads. Make certain each ad you place contains an offer, your phone number and your website's internet address.

Trouble Making
Payroll
This Week?
If your business is having trouble making payroll due to slow paying customers... WE CAN HELP!
Call James the Payroll Pro at (000) 000-0000
or
Visit www.******.com for our FREE 2015 Payroll Finance Report

Payroll
is Friday and NO CHECKS IN THE MAIL?
We Finance Your Accounts Receivable!
Call James the Payroll Pro at (000) 000-0000
or
Visit www.******.com for our FREE 2015 Payroll Finance Report

Need Quick Cash for This Week's
Payroll
Let Our Payroll Pro HELP! WE FINANCE YOUR ACCOUNTS RECEIVABLE
Call James the Payroll Pro at (000) 000-0000
or
Visit www.******.com for our FREE 2015 Payroll Finance Report

Glenco Naples

Business Finance Consultants

Glenn Johnson, a Naples, FL based bookkeeper started *Glenco Consultants* on his 30th birthday. *Glenco* was to provide a new service to Johnson's existing clients, that of sourcing factoring and small business finance. Johnson also felt the new finance arm would provide a good marketing niche to attract more clients to his bookkeeping service.

Johnson's bookkeeping business was doing well and he actually had little time to do any real marketing for the new company. He had developed a knowledge of factoring through a study course provided by the International Association of Commercial Finance Brokers (IACFB) and felt he knew enough to begin offering the service.

To test the "marketing waters" Johnson decided to place a small classified ad about PAYROLL FINANCE in a local shopper-style weekly newspaper. The total cost was just $35 per insertion and he agreed to run the ad four consecutive weeks to get a small discount.

Though he got nothing the first week, Johnson was very surprised to get not one but two inquiries the second week of the ad. One was a very small company making sea shell novelties for sale in various Florida gift shops. The other was a painting contractor who painted apartment interiors for local complexes. The complex management companies paid very slowly. Both small businesses needed factoring.

Johnson introduced both companies to factor in Tampa, FL and factoring arrangements were quickly set in place. While the sea shell novelty company was a very small client doing less than $15,000 per month in factoring, the painting contractor invoiced well over $100,000 per month. Additionally, once the contractor had a factoring arrangement in place, it began to grow rapidly and soon was invoicing between $150,000 - $175,000 each month. Johnson's monthly commission check from the factor averaged well over $750.00 or about $9,000 per year.

Johnson continued with his classified ad program but had little success until nearly 6 months later when he generated another quality lead that resulted in an account with a staffing company that had just opened in the area.

Where to Run Classifieds for Factoring

A cost / benefit analysis on classifieds is eye-opening and they are a great campaign choice for those just starting out. Additionally, there are literally thousand of publications where you can run them. Placing classifieds can certainly be a little "hit or miss", but doing some background work on the publications you intend to advertise in will boost the amount of leads your classified ad campaigns generate. Here are some tips when choosing a publication.

THOUSANDS OF PUBLICATIONS

- Make sure the publication has a well laid out classified section. Publications with just one or two pages of classifieds show limited readership.
- View the types of businesses advertising in the publication. If the publication has a lot of ads placed by service sector companies such as staffing, janitorial, guard, maintenance, etc., it is good publication for your ad.
- All advertisers will view their ads to make sure they were inserted correctly. When viewing theirs, make certain they can see yours. Look carefully at how you can place your ad so business owners can easily see it.
- Study the winners. When looking at a publication's classified section, make note of which ads immediately draw your attention. Mimic those ads, their type face, size, etc. when placing your ad.

STUDY THE WINNERS

Exploring Online Classifieds

Classified ads tend to reach people that are already shopping and one of the most economical methods of getting at such shoppers is online classifieds. Before getting too involved with online classified advertising, be aware you are also opting in to the classified site's newsletters and advertisements. Be prepared to receive such email.

Online classifieds are worth the time and they are a great way to build your own mailing / newsletter list. Many factoring brokers have generated quality leads from online sites such as *Craig's List* and while advertising in that particular online venue is no longer free in many larger cities, in smaller cities it continues without cost.

Holding Informative Workshops

HAS NO EQUAL

Those interested in quickly revving up their new consulting business and putting immediate clients on the books have an exceptional tool at their disposal for doing so...hosting informative workshops and seminars. For garnering immediate response, this method of marketing simply has no equal. In fact, almost every other type of marketing tends to pale in comparison. If you're in a hurry to start generating some of the industry's legendary commission income, workshops and seminars are by far the single best way of doing it.

MANY TOOLS FOR A SINGLE PURPOSE

One of the reasons for the success in generating clients with workshops is that workshop marketing utilizes so many different tools, all focused on a single purpose. It is "guerrilla marketing" at its finest. Each part in the process of holding a workshop supports the others. When holding a workshop, you will "touch" each attendee at least eight different ways including:

⇒ **DIRECT MAIL:** in the form of "invitations" targeted to a specific business group such as service sector companies.

⇒ **YOUR WEBSITE:** and its "invitation page" where those receiving your invitation and responding can reserve their seat and download information.

⇒ **WARM CALLING:** by placing a telephone call to each recipient to either confirm their attendance or to ask if they received your "personal" invitation.

⇒ **CONFIRMATION CALL:** done the day before or day of the workshop as a reminder to the attendee.

⇒ **PUBLIC SPEAKING:** when you make your presentation to your group of target business owners or referral sources.

⇒ **FOLLOW UP TO ATTENDEES:** follow up with a call after the presentation. Get specific about the attendee's business.

⇒ **FOLLOW UP TO THOSE WHO COULD NOT ATTEND:** follow up with the no-shows and those that could not attend. Try booking them for the next workshop.

⇒ **NEWSLETTER:** continued direct-response marketing to both attendees and no-shows.

Tools You Will Need for Workshops

To get into the "workshop marketing" business, you will need certain supplies and pieces of equipment. In many cases, the provider of your lecture room can provide some of these. In other cases, you are going to need to supply everything. What you will need includes:

- a laptop computer
- a projector (visit www.dell.com)
- table top presentation screen (visit www.draperinc.com)
- Microsoft's *PowerPoint* software
- a presentation package (presentation folders, brochures, handouts, etc.)
- an easel with flip chart and markers

Types of Workshops You Can Hold

DIFFERENT VENUES TO REACH CERTAIN AUDIENCES

All of your workshops will naturally be on factoring and small business finance but there are several venues you will use to reach certain audiences. Some will be perfect for your earliest ventures into workshop marketing. Others will be difficult to promote until you fill and grow your prospect lists with sufficient names of small business owners to invite. Here are some examples:

- **BREAKFAST / CLIENT:** These are probably one of the most expensive and poorest choices, especially when you are just starting out. You will need to reserve a room at a local restaurant and provide the meal. Think $8-$10+ dollars per attendee, 20% gratuity, plus a modest room charge. Invitees will be from your compiled lists.
- **LUNCHEON / CLIENT:** Luncheon seminars are relatively modest when it comes to cost. Do NOT, however, hold these in a restaurant. Here you can offer subs and soft drinks that you purchase for about $5 per attendee. Luncheon seminars tend to be the best attended since everyone likes a break in their day for lunch anyway and your seminar gives them a place to learn something while they eat for free. Invitees will be from your compiled lists.

- **AFTER HOURS / CLIENT:** These you will hold after 6:30 pm since attendees will need to get through rush hour traffic to be present. Attendance will usually be lower than luncheon workshops and costs can be all across the board. Invitees will usually be from your prospective client lists which can include databank lists or compiled lists.

- **EDC / SBDC / REFERRAL:** Workshops you provide in concert with Economic Development Corporations (EDC), Small Business Development Corporations (SBDC) or almost any other local business incubator will usually focus on start-up entrepreneurs. Often, you will simply be asked to be a guest speaker at a scheduled monthly meeting such business owners.

  HONE YOUR SMALL GROUP SPEAKING SKILLS

  For new factoring brokers, these incubator workshops are a good place to learn. They provide you with a great opportunity to hone your small group speaking skills. Since they are held at the EDC /SBDC facility, there are usually no costs involved or equipment required. You simply need to have your presentation on a flash drive and an adequate supply of handout packages. You may agree to provide pizza, sandwiches or a similar inexpensive lunch item, but either way, the cost is minimal or nothing at all.

- **SPECIALTY PRESENTATIONS / GUEST SPEAKERSHIPS:** There are dozens of unique groups of business owners or organizations always looking for a guest speaker for their pre-scheduled monthly get-togethers. These include local SCORE Chapters, Community Civic Clubs (*Kiwanis*, *Lions*, *Rotary*, etc.), and local trade groups or organizations. Being asked to speak at such organizations or groups is another perfect opportunity to develop your presentation skills and at the same time, foster some good relationships.

  Civic clubs, such as those mentioned above, are filled with small business owners, accounting professionals, bankers, etc. and can be a great source of both referrals and clients. Similar to the incubators, many will also have all the electronics and equipment you require other than a flip chart. You will simply need to bring your presentation on a flash drive along with your handouts.

When and Where to Hold Workshops

NOTES

When it comes to what time of day to hold your workshops, it really comes down to just a little common sense.

- **EXAMPLE / JANITORIAL SERVICES:** If you are going to give a presentation to a group of janitorial services providers, do NOT schedule an after hours workshop. Commercial janitorial companies clean their customer's buildings after the day is over. They will not be able to attend your after hours event.
- **EXAMPLE / SUB-CONTRACTORS:** If you are going to hold a workshop for sub-contractors, it must be held after hours. Most go to work way too early to attend a breakfast meeting and are likely a bit too dirty to be comfortable for a lunch event. An evening workshop is perfect for this group.
- **EXAMPLE / DISTRIBUTORS:** The time of the workday for manufacturers and distributors is lunch. By noon, they are looking for a little relief from their hectic day and your workshop gives them the perfect informative break.
- **TUESDAYS, WEDNESDAYS, THURSDAYS:** Always hold your events during the middle of the week. Mondays can be too hectic and attendance will be poor. By Friday, most small business entrepreneurs will only have the weekend on their minds.

TUESDAYS WEDNESDAYS THURSDAYS ONLY

- **RESTAURANTS vs. HOTELS / MOTELS:** Holding a workshop event in a restaurant can be expensive and to keep costs under control, you'll need to do some research and shopping. Some facilities will provide the meeting room for free, as long as you spend a minimum amount for food. Hotels and standard motels are usually identical. Many major hotel chains and motels now have "lite" versions for travelers. They are typically featured as "Suites" or "Inns". Such properties have good meeting rooms and economical meeting room rental prices. They will supply water and coffee but often do not have restaurants. This means you can supply the food, such as inexpensive sandwiches, as well as the liquid refreshments.

LOOK TO INNS OR SUITES FOR ROOMS

Showcase Benefits & Deal With Objections

When holding a workshop, seminar or just networking for that matter, you will naturally showcase the benefits of factoring, but you may also have to deal with objections which can arise. Here's how to do it.

The benefits of factoring business accounts receivable are relatively simple for anyone to see and understand. They include:

- **UNLIMITED CAPITAL:** Factoring is the only source of business funding which is unlimited. A factoring facility grows in size as business grows. The more quality invoices a business can generate, the larger the factoring facility.
- **NO DEBT:** Factoring is not a loan so no debt is incurred. It is an "off balance sheet" transactions which can be important to larger manufacturers and distributors.

NO PERSONAL GUARANTEES

- **NO PERSONAL GUARANTEES:** Business owners do not have to personally guaranty any debt.
- **PROFESSIONAL COLLECTIONS:** Factors are courteous collectors of overdue payments. This can free up back office staff for other important duties.
- **CREDIT ANALYSIS:** Factors will screen and monitor the credit of both new and existing customers. This is an important task which can prove very difficult for a small business owner to accomplish alone.
- **FASTER INVOICE PAYMENTS:** Factors typically report their collection experience to *Dun & Bradstreet*. This will help to build a customer's credit history so long as they pay timely. Customers know this and will often go out of their way to pay factored invoices before others.

EASILY ACCESSED

- **READY, EASILY ACCESSED FUNDS:** Unlike a typical bank loan where the business owner's credit is of primary importance, factors are much more concerned about the creditworthiness of the customers of a business. This makes factoring an easily accessed form or ready cash for new, early stage business owners with limited credit history.
- **ELIMINATION OF BAD DEBT:** Under non-recourse factoring arrangements, factors will assume the risk of non-payment from customers, thus eliminating bad debt.

Showcasing the benefits of factoring is relatively simple. The primary "hot buttons" when marketing to business owners are factoring's accessibility as a financing source when the banks say "NO!" and the immediate availability of cash for payroll, supplier payments, and other expenses.

NOTES

ABOUT THE SAME AS TAKING A CREDIT CARD

Objections to factoring are usually based on imperceptions and there are really only three. Most often, these will come from professionals who should know better, such as accountants.

- **FACTORING IS EXPENSIVE:** You will very often have an accounting professional say something like: *"Factoring? That's way too expensive for my clients. Factors charge over 30% per year!"* Accountants should know better and its up to you to point it out, in a nice way of course.

  Factoring is a "transactional" method of financing very similar to accepting credit cards for payment. The average fee for factoring is about 2.5% for 30 days. The average fee for a not-on-premises credit card swipe is about 2.3%. So for the business owner, the costs of factoring for 30 days and the costs of accepting a payment by credit card are virtually the same. When you add in all the other benefits of factoring, its easy to see why it is often the chosen method of payment by many small business owners. Its true that factoring is more expensive than a bank loan, but so are credit cards. And if the business could get a bank loan, it wouldn't need either.

- **FACTORING FACILITIES SHRINK AS BUSINESS SHRINKS:** This is true and is the opposite of the expansion of credit as a business grows. The reality is, factoring is a great method of finance for fast growing businesses. If your business is shrinking, you are less likely to need as much factoring.

- **NOTIFICATION:** Some business owners perceive the notification process as sending a signal to customers that the business is experiencing financial difficulties. This, however, is seldom the case. Factoring notifications are usually written in such a way that conveys the need for factoring as one for a business enjoying "explosive growth" and because of their exceptional credit rating, the business was able to secure the services of a factor to assist in such times of expansion.

Twillie & Associates

Business Finance Consultants

Carlie Twillie is a factoring consultant in St. Louis, MO who focuses 100% of her lead-generation efforts on networking and workshop marketing. When starting her business several years back, Carlie immediately joined a local *Toastmasters Club* so she could improve her public speaking capabilities. Within a short time at *Toastmasters*, she had lost all of her fear of public speaking.

Carlie realized the importance of building relationships with bankers for referral and created a "bankers" group in her CRM and built a list of local community banks. Her goal was to make as many presentations to this group as possible so she could begin building productive referral relationships. She also quickly developed a plan to reach them.

Carlie created a special "invitation page" in her website titled "luncheon.html". She began using direct mail invitations addressed to the local bank presidents offering to host an informative luncheon workshop on factoring for all bank employees. For convenience, it was to be held in the bank's boardroom. Carlie would supply lunch and refreshments from a local sub shop.

To get the bankers to respond, Carlie utilized a great little direct mail trick: *Invitation Cards.* She modified the very same type of heavy stock card used to invite guests to a party. Each invitation was hand addressed and featured a commemorative stamp rather than machine postage. The cards were very simple. On the front it said "*A Special Invitation for You*". On the inside it said, *"Please visit www.CTwillieAssoc.com/luncheon.html".*

Every component of a direct mail package has a job. The job of the envelope is simply to get opened. One hundred percent of Carlie's envelopes were opened due to their unique appearance. Using the website analytics installed on her website, she found that over 90% of the bankers receiving her invitation also made the journey to her site's special invitation page.

Her invitation page, luncheon.html, utilized some good graphics and featured a short presentation package with a PDF download she had designed. The PDF package contained several great case studies and an explanation of how factoring and alternative commercial finance could help with business customer retention at small community banks.

The results of even her first small mailing were impressive. She was able to book three presentations for the following month....a marketing coup for *Twillie & Associates*.

Marketing with Direct Mail

NOTES

Utilizing traditional direct mail marketing tends to produce poor results for most factoring brokers. And, it can be a bit expensive when you include all its components. If using a standard #10 envelope, brochure, and sales letter, it is unusual to get even a 1% response rate on large bulk mailing campaigns.

Direct mail does have its uses for factoring brokers, however, and it can be used powerfully as seen in the preceding example. You just need to be a little creative in how its used. Here are a few tips when using direct mail for your consulting business.

- Never use a regular #10 envelope. Too many such "normal" mailings simply find their way into the circular file.
- Always hand address envelopes if possible. Add your personal touch. If your handwriting is terrible, employ someone that comes equipped with that skill.
- Use special commemorative stamps and never machine postage. Commemorative stamps are available from your local post office and you'll have many movie stars, famous people and depictions of historical events to choose from. They cost no more than regular postage.
- Only use direct mail to drive the receiver to your website for an offer. Direct mail and your website make a potent team. It is very easy, using *Google Analytics,* to measure the response rates of your direct mail campaigns.
- Make the size of your direct mail campaigns manageable. Always plan on following up each piece of direct mail with a personal call to the recipient. This will no longer be a pure cold call but rather a "warm" call since your mail (if opened) has softened up the prospect.

ALWAYS HAND ADDRESS MAIL

USE COMMEMORATIVE STAMPS

Good uses for direct mail by factoring brokers tend to focus around special events or unique offerings. For example, your newsletter marketing program can utilize a monthly e-newsletter but feature a print newsletter once each quarter or twice a year. Use the direct mail newsletter special print version for "local distribution only". Your e-newsletter can be received by the masses.

DIRECT MAIL NEWSLETTERS

Direct Mail & Disaster Funding

CUSTOMER PAYMENTS SLOW DOWN MARKEDLY

Another great time to use direct mail for marketing is during some catastrophic event. Factors are very quick to adapt to changing circumstances and when natural disasters occur, factors can provide ready funding to small businesses within hours. One of the reasons factoring is so necessary during such events is that customer payments tend to slow down markedly, a perfect time to employ factoring. Floods, tornadoes, hurricanes, wildfires, blizzards, drought, etc. all provide excellent opportunities to market your professional consulting services via direct mail. You can even find such marketing opportunities by visiting www.fema.gov

When marketing in a community ravaged by a disastrous occurrence, you may not be able to depend on your website for support. Often after such events, the infrastructure is damaged to the extent that internet access will be unavailable for weeks or even months. Under such circumstances, it will be direct mail and only direct mail that carries your message.

NOTORIOUSLY SLOW IN PAYING

In many cases of natural disaster, FEMA will be present (Federal Emergency Management Agency) and while disaster funds will be made available, FEMA is notoriously slow in paying its bills. Businesses tendering invoices to FEMA for reimbursement can often expect to wait 90-120 days or longer until receiving payment.

For freelance brokers interested in employing direct mail marketing, mailing to businesses suffering from a recent disastrous event can lead to booking some very profitable new accounts. This is one of the few areas where direct mail will be the number one choice for delivering your message. To use direct mail for such occurrences:

PURCHASE A LIST BY ZIP CODE

- Purchase a list of business in the area selling B2B. Order the list by ZIP codes affected by the event.
- Create a good cover letter offering your services and include your latest brochure.
- Include a plastic *Rolodex card* in each envelope. Have the heading tab on the card printed to read: "*Disaster Funding*".

HAMMERWHISTLE
& ASSOCIATES

Commercial Finance Consultants

Belinda Hammerwhistle (Bell) is a factoring consultant and has operated *Hammerwhistle & Associates* in Port St. Lucie, FL for 9 years. Bell is always on the lookout for unique business development opportunities and immediately took notice when a local news broadcaster reported a story on a large Gulf oil spill which was going to impact the Florida coastline. It is well known that such natural disasters almost always expose opportunities for landing new factoring accounts as local small business owners struggle in the disaster's aftermath.

Bell knew from previous experience that hundreds of part-time workers would be needed to assist in beach clean up once the oil began to wash ashore. Many of these workers would be sourced through local staffing companies. Bell also knew that in such disasters, FEMA and other very slow paying emergency relief organizations would become involved and the local staffing companies would require ready sources of funding to be able to bridge the time gap between the payment of the weekly payroll for the temporary help and the slow release of cleanup reimbursement funds by the emergency relief organizations. It was a perfect opportunity to bring in some new factoring clients.

Bell had ordered some plastic rolodex cards for just such occasional "disasters" some years back and although the idea of using rolodex cards seemed a bit antiquated in today's electronic age, they worked perfectly for these "special" campaigns. The cards were made of thin red plastic and featured a tab at the top that simply said "DISASTER FUNDING". The body of the card had all of Bell's contact information along with her web address.

Bell quickly bought a mailing list of staffing companies using zip codes located along the beach areas where the oil was due to come ashore and did an immediate direct mail campaign of 500 pieces. Over the next 30 days she opened two new factoring accounts for staffing companies and had several referrals for area construction cleanup companies making this $300 mailing one the most successful in her 9 year history in the industry.

More Opportunities for Direct Mail

When talking direct mail, most visualize blanketing large lists of prospects with thousands of pieces and advertisements. But the costs of such mailings are really prohibitive even with the earnings potential of a single factoring account. This is especially true when you consider the average direct mail response rate is just 1/10 of one percent. To justify using direct mail in mass quantities, you will need a response rate 20 times that amount.

Factoring brokers that use direct mail successfully tend to use a much more personalized version on a much smaller scale, as in our previous example of "disaster marketing". Other perfect opportunities will involve using direct mail in combination with other media to promote a FREE OFFER of some kind. For example, use direct mail to:

- Invite members of your compiled list to one of your upcoming workshops. (always follow up with a phone call)
- Contact small groups of brand new business owners in your area with a B2B factoring example. (always follow up with phone call)
- Follow up on local promotions and giveaways you're involved in.
- Announce a "Special Guest" teleconference. (always follow up with a phone call and also announce this event in your newsletter)
- Invite business owners to sponsored events. (drive them to your website for more detailed information)
- Announce a special offer on your website. Direct mail is much more efficient than email for such promotions. If you have authored a booklet on small business finance, for example, make it available in PDF format for download on your website's invitation page. Announce this offer to your compiled list with invitation mailers. Track the results with website analytics. Add those that respond to your response list (prospect list).

CAMELTHORPE
& ASSOCIATES

Commercial Finance Consultants

"Cam" Camelthorpe is a retired postal worker in Biloxi, MS and was looking for a good home-based business to start to provide some additional part-time income for himself and his wife in retirement. When he stumbled upon factoring and commercial finance consulting, he knew that was perfect for him.

Although living in Biloxi, Cam grew up in Green Bay, WI and has always been a *Packers* fan. Every Sunday during season, he religiously dons some green and gold and heads to the *Didgeridoo Saloon and Sports Bar,* a local sports hangout, to watch games. He has met dozens of other *Green Bay* fans including some bankers and accounting professionals. Cam is a very creative "marketeer" and has turned almost every personal pastime he has into a marketing event of some kind for his new business. He thought these recurring Sunday meetups would be a good addition. So he began putting together a creative sponsorship for his consultancy, *Camelthorpe & Associates.*

Cam negotiated a deal with the owners of the *Didgeridoo Saloon* to show the *Packers* game on the bar's largest big screen television along with sound. The condition was that Cam needed to produce at least 20 *Green Bay* fans in the group every Sunday to get the "special treatment". Cam knew that would be easy and he quickly designed a program that he felt would do the job. His single goal for this marketing campaign was to drive visitors to his business website so they could learn more about him and his business.

Cam got his web designer to create a new page for his site called "invitation-gb.html". This would be the new landing page for his direct mail marketing campaign. He then arranged for a local print shop to prepare some classy invitation cards with a football helmet on the front. The inside simply said; "You're Invited. Visit www.camelthorpeassoc.com/invitation-gb.html"

Each week Jim would promote the event by giving away a jersey, cap, block of Wisconsin cheddar, or similar prize. His webpage announced the weekly winner and became the source for group's local updates. Jim would mail cards to prospective new participants when he was referred a name and address by another member. He had already met nearly a dozen *Green Bay* fans simply by networking at local after hours Chamber meetings and had built a special "group category" in his CRM just for this campaign. He kept fans up to date through an email blast every week which had a hot link directly to his special invitation page.

His weekly football fan sponsorship has provided Cam with the opportunity to build relationships with several bankers and accounting professionals in the group. He has also been asked many questions about his business and services by other members. Cam knows clients or client referrals will just be a matter of time.

Holding "Special Guest" Teleconferences

Another opportunity which can be marketed through direct mail is when the factoring broker holds a "*Special Guest Teleconference*". This is a great tool for list building and especially when you are new to the industry. Who is your special guest? Why a factor of course.

When you first begin to work with a factor or a factor's BDO, see if they would be interested in being the special guest speaker on a teleconference you arrange. Marketing using such teleconferences is much like workshop marketing, just a little less effective. There are no expense to holding such teleconferences other than the direct mail marketing required to get the attendees on the call.

When holding *Special Guest Teleconferences*, the broker really has just three tasks which are to:

MAKE SURE THE CONFERENCE CALL IS FILLED

- **Introduce the speaker (factor or BDO) to the audience**
- **Make sure the teleconference is filled with attendees**
- **Moderate the teleconference**

The second job is obviously the most critical. Most factors will gladly be a guest speaker and make a 15 - 30 minute presentation IF you can fill the conference with attendees. The magic number you want here is 25-30 small business owners to make everyone happy. If you fail to perform and don't bring in the numbers, the factor or BDO will probably take little interest in speaking a second time.

50% DROPOUTS AND NO-SHOWS

To meet the minimum requirement of attendees, you will need about 60 people that actually respond to your invitation and R.S.V.P. they will attend. In other words, expect about 50% no-shows and drop outs for your presentation.

When moderating, simply make a good introduction of the factor and his firm and then step out. Get attendees to mute themselves while listening so there is no background noise. If some do not mute, then you can mute the audience from your phone to make certain your guest can be heard. To close, thank everyone for attending. Make certain you email a list of attendees to the factor.

Creative Sponsorships

NOTES

When you sponsor something, you are financially supporting a person, organization, or cause. Sponsorships are considered to be the fastest growing form of marketing in the U.S. and also represent one of the most powerful networking and relationship building tools for your factoring and commercial finance consulting business. Recognizing good opportunities for sponsorships and arranging to participate in them will allow you to meet and network with very large numbers of potential referral sources and even prospective clients all at one time.

FASTEST GROWING FORM OF MARKETING

Though sponsorships often involve some form of charitable cause or philanthropic event, the financial contribution of the sponsor is almost always provided with some financial benefit in mind. In other words, sponsors expect a "payback" for their support and a great example of such payback would be the "*Bankers Bash*".

SPONSORS EXPECT A PAYBACK

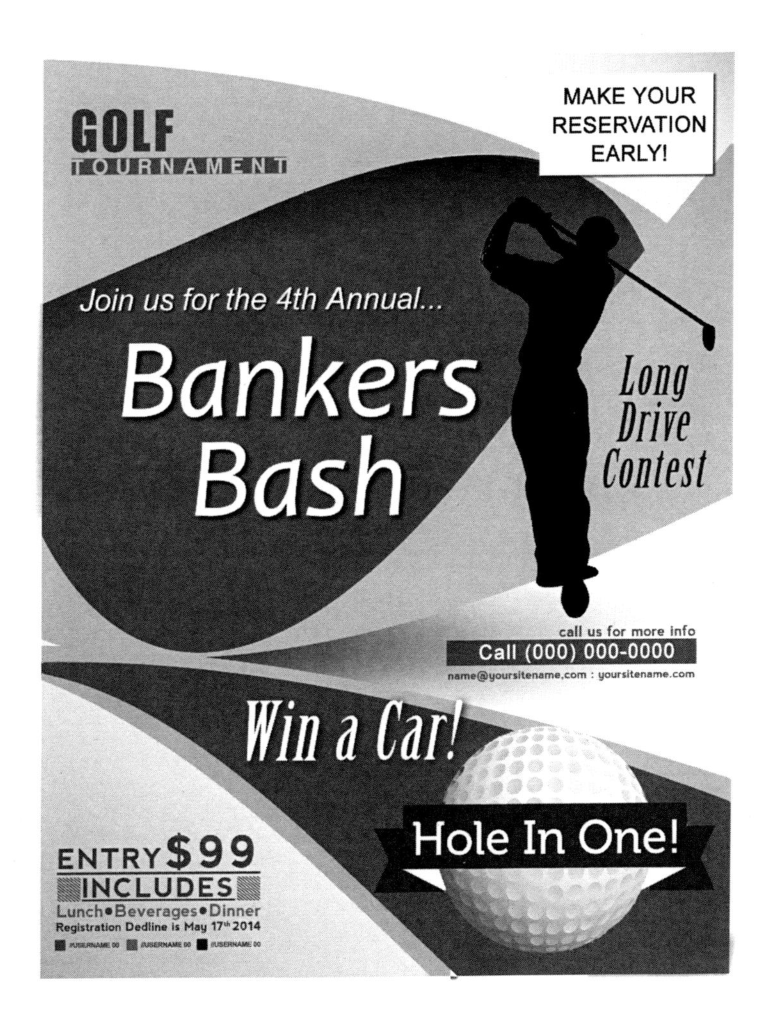

PROMOTIONAL GIVAWAYS

Bill, a factoring broker, belongs to a popular service club in his community and over time, has worked his way into a position of leadership and authority. One of the club's primary annual fundraisers is something called the "*Bankers Bash*", a charitable golf tournament made up of teams strictly from the local banking community. Bill has worked hard to get put in charge of the *BASH.* He knew it meant having the opportunity to meet and build relationships with dozens of local loan officers and other bank employees each year. Once in charge and in typical "Bill" fashion, he decided to make the *BASH* bigger and more popular than ever. He was going to give away a car by having his company sponsor a "Hole-In-One" contest.

Bill contacted an insurance company that offered promotional hole-in-one insurance and found he could purchase an insurance policy for about $1,000. The insurance would cover the cost of a popular $40,000 German import in the event a participant made a hole-in-one. This was well within Bill's annual marketing budget so he quickly purchased the insurance for the event. After a call or two, he found the local import auto dealer was more than happy to have one of his bright red sport coupes on display at the event which would be parked right on the on the grass next to the par 3's tee box. As an added bonus, the dealer even offered to pick up half the cost of the $1,000 insurance policy.

Although Bill was an avid golfer, he did not play in his own event. Instead, he set up shop right on the par 3's tee box so he could meet, greet, and shake hands with every banker as they tried to win the car. He had coolers of refreshments available and gave each contestant a free sleeve of "lucky" golf balls with his company's name and a four leaf clover boldly imprinted on each ball.

The Bottom Line

The "BASH" was a networking and relationship building BONANZA for Bill!

- Prior to the "BASH", Bill visited every bank in the area, passing out entry forms and invitations to play in the tournament. And...meeting loan officers while doing so.
- At the tournament, Bill personally shook hands with each player, gave them a logoed gift, and wished them luck on winning the car HIS COMPANY was giving away.
- Over the next several weeks, Bill stopped in every bank that fielded a team, thanked the bank officers personally, handed out "leftover" promotional items with his company's logo, and began the relationship process by inviting them to have lunch sometime.

Community Recognition Benefits

Sponsorships can be a great way to give a little back to your community. They are also a great way for you and your business to become a community topic of conversation. Whether you hit a home run, as in the previous *Bankers Bash* example, or simply get on base with a few singles and smaller ideas, sponsorships can provide fertile ground for growing relationships and joining the ranks of your community's movers and shakers.

JOIN THE RANKS OF MOVERS & SHAKERS

As mentioned, good sponsorships for your consideration should provide you with recognition, and we don't mean having your name along with hundreds of others in miniscule type at the bottom of a event program. Good sponsorships are geared to opportunities which are *quid pro quo.* From your standpoint, there must be a way provided for local business owners or referral sources to know about your generous participation in the event.

In some cases, such quality exposure can be generated by you. For example, have your webmaster create an area on your website which features your company's advocacy or volunteerism. If you routinely work for *Habitat for Humanity* building homes, for example, have a photo album of pictures of your recent projects on your site. You can feature an article about upcoming projects in your newsletter and provide a direct link to your website's photo album. The goal here is to create an awareness of you and your company.

CREATE AWARENESS FOR YOU AND YOUR COMPANY

Here are some guidelines when considering a sponsorship:

- Will this event give you exposure to B2B business owners?
- Will you have the opportunity to be included in the event's publicity?
- Can you comfortably afford it?
- Will participating in this event provide you with quality networking opportunities and good sources of referral?

Sponsorships can be excellent ways to generate interest in your business while at the same time providing an outlet for your need to do good. Just make certain there is real benefit in your investment.

Expert Status Through Authoring

If you are a reasonably good writer and enjoy it, you will find many local publications which will be interested in publishing interesting articles you write on small business finance and factoring. Often, these can be the very same publications where you are placing your classified ads, giving you a real one-two marketing punch.

SAME PUBLICATIONS AS FOR CLASSIFED ADVERTISEMENTS

Writing articles, columns, and case studies will help you to reach one of your primary goals as a factoring broker, which is being locally recognized as an industry expert. It gives you local visibility and a lot of it if your articles appear in the right publications.

Writing Informative Articles

Writing short, interesting articles on factoring and small business finance is a great place to start your authoring career. In almost any locale, there are dozens of small advertising-focused publications looking for informative "filler" content. A majority of such small publications are free to the public. They generate 100% of their revenue from the placement of small business ads and will have an active classified section.

LOOKING FOR FILLER CONTENT

Do your research. These magazines can be found outside of your local grocery stores, retail stores, and restaurants in great numbers. Grab a few copies and page through them when the opportunity permits. Look at the article content and get a feel for what the magazine is looking for. Go to the magazine's website and research submission guidelines. View sample article length and see if it seems like a fit for you. If the magazine feels like a good match, query the editor.

It is very easy to query the editors of these small publications to determine their interest. Don't get upset with a "no" or no response at all. There are several ways around this and if you cannot move around it there are dozens of other publications where you can find interest in your article.

Sample Query Letter

NOTES

Below is a sample query letter to use for your article submissions.

From: (Your Name)
To: (Editor's Complete Name & Job Title)
Subject: Query Letter
Email Address: (Editor's Email Address)

Hello (Editor's First Name)

Our local small business owners are faced with many challenges in today's economy. One of the greatest is locating ready sources of working capital for normal operations and sustained growth.

Small business entrepreneurs, and especially many B2B operators such as your advertisers, are often faced with an inability to secure traditional bank financing due to their short time in business, a lack of meaningful collateral, or a slightly tarnished credit history. But many small B2B business owners are learning of a powerful option available to them, regardless of their credit history or time in business. ACCOUNTS RECEIVABLE FACTORING!

Would a feature article on factoring and its ability to provide financing for small businesses be a good fit for (Magazine Name)? *Factoring is one of the simplest forms of commercial finance available to entrepreneurial enterprise. I foresee this article addressing:*

- *the well known cash flow problems your small business readers face*
- *how factoring can quickly address those problems*
- *why factoring is so readily accessible to small business owners*

(Editor's First Name), *I am a freelance small business finance consultant and specialize in providing small business finance solutions to very young "start up" ventures and minority business enterprise.*

I look forward to hearing your feedback. Thank you in advance for your consideration.

Your First Name, Last Name, & Email Address
Website Domain

Writing a Column

If an editor accepts one of your article submissions, talk to them about a periodic column on small business finance. The column does not need to be weekly or even monthly, just periodic. Landing this appointment will not only set you up as a recognized expert in your community, but will also give you excellent opportunities for networking.

Writing a periodic column for a small local publication will require that you address financing alternatives other than just factoring. And to get the latest up-to-date information for your column, you will naturally need to meet with and interview:

- **Members of your local SCORE**
- **Officers of your local SBDC and EDC**
- **Bank Loan Officers**
- **Officers of other local incubators**
- **CPAs and accountants**

EXCELLENT NETWORKING OPPORTUNITIES

In other words, becoming a column writer will give you immediate and almost unlimited access to important contacts in your small business finance community. These are the very same people you are trying as hard as you can to meet and network with at local Chamber of Commerce events. The difference is, they are now just a phone call and interview away.

Additionally, writing a column not only provides you will expert status, it also gives you "credentials". You will become a welcome and known celebrity guest at every area financial function.

Start a Blog

Writing a column can naturally lead to starting your own small business finance blog. Blogging is incredibly popular and its really relatively easy to set up and start a blog with *Word Press.* Though easy, you will need to do a little research on this subject since it is beyond the scope of this book to detail. It represents an exceptional opportunity, however, to once again elevate yourself as an expert.

Writing Case Studies

NOTES

Case studies can provide detailed examples of how factoring can be utilized to deal with a particular small business cash flow problem. They are relatively easy to prepare and you have already seen many examples of case studies in this guide.

USED AS AN OFFER

When marketing, factoring case studies are commonly used as an offer and part of a direct mail campaign. The receiver is able to download the case study after visiting your website and completing an opt-in form. The report is then dispensed through your website as a PDF.

Case studies are also an important component of your handout packages when holding workshops and seminars. They are a very compelling tool which can be easily created or modified to address problems of a specific target group.

TWO CASE STUDIES ON YOUR WEBSITE

Most factoring consultants will always have at least two case studies featured on their website at any given time.

1. The first will typically be more like a small booklet which explains factoring to any visitor which passively happens upon the site. It will be a bit generic, but may include several good examples of how factoring works, the costs involved, etc.
2. The second will be more specific and will be housed in the site's invitation or "squeeze" page. This case study should have a direct correlation to a specific type of business such as a janitorial service, staffing company, etc. Those accessing this particular case study will have received an email or invitational piece of direct mail with the specific URL for the page.

Though it does not have to be done immediately, you will need to write a good selection of case studies to always have on hand. When meeting and networking with a new owner of a guard service, for example, it will be very beneficial if you can say; "*By the way, I have a great little report on financing alternatives for guard services just like yours. Would you like me to a email a free copy to you?*"

The Power of Networking

All factoring brokers with an eye on success will become heavily involved in networking and relationship building. And rightfully so, since over 50% of all new accounts are sourced simply as a matter of referral. All types of businesses can benefit from networking. Your business of brokering factoring transactions actually thrives on it.

Networking and relationship building is often called "Word of Mouth" marketing. It is a "keystone" of your inbound marketing efforts. On the upside, it will be much less costly than direct marketing (an often important trait for those first entering the industry), but on the downside, it will likely take longer for you to see commission-generating results if you use it exclusively.

For those entering the industry on a part time basis, networking may be the perfect low budget business development strategy for you to implement while getting started. If you're entering with more of a career focus, using networking as an exclusive source of lead generation will probably be quickly recognized as being a bit too slow. Even for full-time freelance professionals, however, it should probably be part of 50 /50 marketing mix that includes various types of direct response campaigns as well.

As you know, your consultant business is all about generating leads and keeping your *response list* full. Direct response call-to-action marketing does this in one quick step, as the name suggests.

- **Place an ad...get a response.**
- **Place a lot of ads...get a lot of responses.**

And of course, some percentage of the responses you receive become clients. Sales is often referred to as a "numbers game" and nothing could be more true. Especially when it comes to direct marketing.

Word-of-mouth marketing is quite a bit different. It is a multi-step process. With word-of-mouth you must:

- meet a person that is a member of a professional group that can either become a client or send referrals your way
- interact with that person, explore mutual interests, and impress them with your expertise
- wait for opportunities to exchange referrals (yes, it works both ways)

When it comes to networking and relationship building, you really need to look at these two processes separately. Although they are definitely a duo, the processes and results are quite different.

THEY ARE DEFINITELY A DUO

- **NETWORKING:** Networking can be defined as any face-to-face contact that may establish a relationship which can lead to business.
- **RELATIONSHIP BUILDING:** Can be defined as a mutual affiliation between two parties. In short, it is a friendship. Networking opens the door for relationship building.

Networking tends to be quick and painless. It "establishes" a momentary relationship. Exchange business cards, converse for a few moments, and then off to the next conquest. Maybe referral business comes from it. Maybe not. But you have sown a seed.

NETWORKING ESTABLISHES A RELATIONSHIP

Relationship building, on the other hand, requires time and effort. It "builds" on the introduction established by networking and takes it to a higher and more beneficial level. It is usually a slow and difficult process, but it is the relationships that you nurture and grow that will be the real source of your referrals and leads.

RELATIONSHIP BUILDING TAKES IT TO A HIGHER LEVEL

Although the use of networking and relationship building will probably account for at least 50% of your time once you have become established, for most brokers it will be a much larger marketing portion when first starting out. We would estimate that networking should probably account for roughly 75%-80% of your time when first opening your doors with traditional outbound direct marketing making up the balance.

75%-80% OF YOUR TIME SHOULD BE SPENT ON NETWORKING

Positioning For Networking

One of the most important considerations in networking is *positioning.* By positioning, we mean making certain you have positioned yourself in the "right" clubs and organizations...those which will yield the best results. Too often new brokers simply join a civic organization with the idea that all are basically the same. That is definitely not true at all.

YOUR CHOICE OF CLUBS

For example, you may decide you want to join a *Rotary Club* and you find there are no less than seven such clubs in your area. *Rotary Clubs* typically only allow one member from each specific vocation per club so newer clubs are started as older clubs get filled up. For you, as a factoring broker, it is likely you will have your choice of clubs. The competition in the industry is actually that light. So which club do you choose?

You will need to do a little research. One club might be located downtown in the courthouse district. It will be full of attorneys (one for each specialty area) and a few other professionals. Another club might be in the industrial district. It will be full of manufacturers, distributors, service providers, etc. and all prospective clients for your services. You can network at both and you can network exactly the same way. But while you might get an eventual referral or two from a room full of attorneys, the opportunities would pale in comparison to a club full of potential small business clients.

So do your research before you join clubs and organizations for your networking adventures. Most clubs will provide you with a sponsor and with a "free look". Come as a guest and view the size of the crowd and what type of members make it up. It can make an enormous difference when it comes to networking and all important referrals. Make certain the networking venues you choose represent truly fertile ground where you will have opportunities to "harvest" results.

Your Networking Advantage

NOTES

When it comes to networking, you will have a natural "advantage" over almost everyone else in the room. At networking events, virtually everyone in the room is there to sell something. Buy mine instead of theirs. Use me instead of her. That is, everyone except you. Your business is one of pure service and not a service of convenience. There is no choice. A business owner either:

- **needs working capital or it doesn't**
- **can obtain bank financing or it can't**

And it's really that simple. You do not compete with banks. You augment banks. You provide services when they can't or choose not to. Your business is one that radiates confidence. Your goal is simply to let those you meet know what you do. You sell nothing. When they need you, you're there.

YOU DO NOT COMPETE WITH BANKS

So when networking, the pressure is off. Everyone else in the room is there to impress everyone else. And while you certainly do want to make bankers and accounting professionals aware of your potent financing knowledge, that's about it. Your product stands alone and you will likely have zero competition.

YOUR PRODUCT STANDS ALONE

When a new acquaintance asks what you do, simply say, I'm in "specialty finance" and pass them your card. Since specialty finance is a bit vague, they will likely ask questions and you can then expand a bit with some details. Ask them what they do and then provide a quick example (mini-case study) of how your services can help. If they are a retailer, you will give an example of merchant cash. If they are B2B, you can use factoring. If they are a large B2B, you can use asset-based lending. If they export, you can use international factoring. You will find you probably have a ready financing tool for everybody in the room.

You should also be prepared to occasionally be the center of attention at networking events and especially around bankers. This is because they are interested in what you do. Most have never really heard of your services. They are curious and will want to know more and to find out how you can help them.

BE PREPARED TO BE THE CENTER OF ATTENTION

How to Follow Up

As you work the room at any networking event, you'll find many business owners who will say, "*I have all the money I need right now*". And, they are probably telling the truth. But, are they a prospect for your services? You bet. In business, the one thing you can be certain of is change and especially when it comes to cash flow. Making the initial contact at a networking event is simply step one. You now need to keep the introduction from going stale. Here's how.

ENTER INFORMATION IN YOUR CRM IMMEDIATELY

After the event, always get the information from those you meet into your CRM. Do it immediately, while details are fresh in your mind. When you add their personal record, also assign them to a "group" you have set up for the networking event. For example, if you meet an accountant at a Chamber of Commerce meet up, create a personal record but also assign it to the "group" called *Chamber of Commerce.* That way, you can scan group members before each subsequent Chamber event to refresh you memory regarding the names of important contacts. Remembering a person's name when you meet a second or third time will impress them. It tells them you are interested in them personally and their business.

Attend meetings regularly. For example, if you met an individual at a specific bi-weekly after hours event, make certain you attend that same event again. Try to "touch" people you have met at least 2 or 3 times.

Send a Personal Business Email

PERSONAL BUSINESS EMAIL

While you are adding the new contact to your CRM, send them a simple email from your business email address. ONLY use your business email such as bill@brokerwebsite.com.

Any short email will do such as:

Great to meet you at the Chamber event last Wednesday. Looks like that's a pretty well attended meetup.

Bill Broker
www.brokerwebsite.com

A business email address is a pretty important "stealth" marketing tool and very inexpensive. In fact, you should probably have two business email addresses associated with your website.

- A general business email such as info@ or contact@
- A personal business email such as bill@ or gina@

USE YOUR PERSONAL BUSINESS EMAIL FOR EVERYHTING

Once created, you should begin using your personal business email for everything. Personal business emails provide a perfect method of letting everyone you know you are in business. Because the email address contains your business website's URL, those that receive your email can easily satisfy their curiosity about your business and what you are up to these days without personally asking you.

Never add those you have met personally to your marketing service email for e-newsletters and bulletins. Once you have met someone face-to-face, you are beyond such generic marketing tools. You now need to utilize direct mail to maintain a periodic relationship-building contact. What you need is a print newsletter.

Touch With Powerful Print Newsletters

Once you begin networking in earnest, you must stay active on your networking circuit. Unfortunately, just because you stay active doesn't mean those you meet stay active as well. And what many networking experts say is this. If you do not "touch" someone you've met at a networking event within a month of your first introduction, any relationship value you initially established is reduced by at least 25%. If you do not interact with them for three months, the seed you planted for a relationship is likely valueless.

So how do you touch those important contacts who are not showing up or have dropped out of your circuit? One of the best ways is with an informative print newsletter.

THE ELEPHANT IN THE ROOM

When it comes to staying in touch with quality prospects and important sources of referral, print newsletters are the elephant in the room. Not only do they provide a medium for showcasing your expert knowledge of business finance through their interesting and informative articles, they also begin setting the stage for building a more meaningful personal relationship.

When it comes to networking, nothing can replace the face-to-face contact found at a live event. But until such opportunities again present themselves, print newsletters can provide a mode of communication which will keep you front and center in a contact's mind.

STAYING POWER AND PASS AROUND VALUE

Good print newsletters are much more than advertisements for your business. They are publications that you, the expert, author. If properly constructed, they will not only have staying power, but also "pass around" value. To take advantage of these two features, you need to make sure your newsletter contains attention-getting local content of interest to readers as well as some case studies and feature articles. Here are some suggestions.

- Readers love to know what's happening locally. Add a calendar column for upcoming local events. These can be of an entertainment or civic in nature.

ADD A POLL

- Add a poll. Your readers want to make their opinions known. Present the poll in your newsletter but let readers take the poll by visiting your website.
- Create a crossword or similar word puzzle. You can post answers to the puzzle in the newsletter or on your website. There is excellent free software on the web that will construct your crossword puzzle for you.
- Add a joke or cartoon. Everyone loves a bit of humor.
- Add a "recipe of the month".
- Add an article on an under-the radar, cool vacation spot.
- Use pictures and graphics liberally. Use at least one graphic per page.
- Add a quote of the month.

So there are many ways to not only make your print newsletter interesting, but also add to its staying power and pass around value. Most experts say the perfect size for a monthly newsletter is 4 pages. That is a single sheet of 17 x 11 paper folded. Software such as *Microsoft Publisher* or *Adobe InDesign* will make publishing a monthly newsletter a breeze and actually fun.

Relationship Building

NOTES

THE ULTIMATE GOAL OF ALL NETWORKING

Relationship building is the ultimate goal of all networking and the most important relationships you need to build are those with bank lending officers, accounting professionals, attorneys, insurance agents, incubator managers, directors of SBDCs, and others. All are highly desirable. None will have more referral potential, however, than commercial lending officers.

When you meet a commercial lending officer, your goal is to advance to a one-on-one meeting and at first, this usually means lunch. It may grow over time to include golf, tennis, family dinners or more. But first, try to arrange a simple lunch meeting.

As you converse you will find out important personal information. Through informal conversation, gather information on the person's:

- Favorite sports and sports teams
- Favorite hobbies
- Family situation. What are the children's names?
- College affiliations
- Residence. How long in the area?
- Favorite vacation and travel spots
- Birthday
- Holiday plans
- Political affiliations

AVOID INTERROGATIONS

The more personal information you can glean during normal conversations, the faster you can find common interests upon which to build a friendship. Make sure, however, you avoid converting an enjoyable lunch between two people into an interrogation. Just make note of the normal conversational content that comes up that provides you with some insight into the person.

Make certain you update the person's record in your CRM as soon as possible after any meeting. It's easy to forget important information even after just a few hours.

CONCLUSIONS

Opportunity Awaits

NOTES

Now that you've finished reading the Factoring 101 training guide, you may be starting to wonder why you didn't discover this unique opportunity 10 or 20 years ago. And, now that you have discovered it, how long will it take to get up and operational? When you are going to officially enter the industry?

For some, entry will be quick and painless. For others it will take some preparation and maybe even some personal upgrading. But for most, it may be just a matter of jumping in and testing the waters. To do so, you really only need three things:

- **KNOWLEDGE:** Take the *Proficiency Exam* located in the IACFB Learning Lab. Take it as many times as necessary until you can score 85% or higher.
- **WEBSITE:** Either build a professional website yourself or engage a designer to do it for you. The Business-in-a-Box option also provides exceptional websites for factoring brokers. Your website is a virtual office and a necessity when you are first starting out.
- **BUSINESS CARDS:** Have 500-1,000 business cards printed with contact info including your web domain.

YOUR WEBSITE: A VIRTUAL OFFICE

Getting Part-Time Operational

One of the most appealing characteristics of brokering factoring transactions is the ability for the consultant to work as much or as little they like. Minimal part-time, maximum full-time, and everything in between. Though we discussed in detail what it takes to enter the industry on a truly professional basis in Chapter 5... *Getting Ready for Business*, many brokers, probably 50% or more, begin their careers in factoring on we could call an "occasional" basis. They test the waters based upon their current skills.

From an outbound marketing standpoint, they may place an occasional classified ad, but that's all. From an inbound marketing standpoint, they network a bit, but only at venues where they currently already belong. They invest very little in their business other than time, until they feel comfortable doing so. In short, they approach the business as minimalists. And for those seeking to enter the industry in such a way, there is good news!

Operating as a "Minimalist"

OPERATING AS A "MINIMALIST"

Consulting is just one of those great professions perfect for part-time participation. There is no need for inventory or a retail counter because your product (knowledge) is in your head. To deliver your product to those in need, you require just two marketing tools. You will need a virtual office (website) and some business cards.

Your costs of operation are staggeringly low. Consider that once your website is built, your costs to operate as a broker on a minimalist basis include:

- **Monthly website hosting fees and annual domain renewal**
- **Replacement business cards**

So once set up, your cost of operation can be just a few dollars each month. When you consider the potential commission income from just one or two clients generated "accidentally" each year by simply being in the right place at the right time, there are very few (if any) part-time businesses that can compare to brokering factoring transactions.

Excitement: Getting Your First Deal

There is little to compare with landing your first brokered deal in factoring. As an industry "newbie", you will likely:

- Grab your calculator and estimate your monthly broker fees (trying hard not to embellish them).
- Multiply that fee by 12 to estimate your annual income from the single deal.
- Divide $100,000 by that figure to determine how many similar deals you'll need to break the $100,000 mark.
- Start planning an exotic vacation.
- Call your mother.
- Call your father.
- Call your ex-wife or ex-husband...the one who told you that you'd never amount to anything.
- Call anyone else you think will listen.
- Ask yourself exactly why you're saddled with $25,000 in student loans for a "puppy farm" education that taught you absolutely nothing about really making money.

One Way Street. No Turning Back!

So you may now be beginning to understand, whether you just dabble a bit in freelance brokering or dive into the industry with career intentions, once you land your first brokered deals you'll be hooked. You now have the knowledge necessary to make BIG money and there's no way to unlearn it. In some form or fashion, from this point on, you'll be a factoring broker for life.

You may even begin to enjoy the attention and status that comes with being a high-profile business finance expert. The professionals you're now mingling with accept you as an equal. They respect you and your unique area of knowledge. The money is there too, for the making. So it is now completely up to you. How long it takes you to begin earning it and truly enjoying the many benefits of this exceptional profession is all on your shoulders.

ONE WAY STREET NO TURNING BACK

Whether you practice on a full-time basis or look at brokering as simply something to do in your spare time, it won't matter one bit. You will now always carry your business cards with you and always maintain a virtual office on the web. You now understand that learning to broker factoring transactions is strictly a one-way street. Once you have the knowledge, there's no turning back.

The Factoring 101 Broker Forums

The *Factoring 101 Broker Forums* were created to provide a place for readers of the *Factoring 101 Training Guide* to ask questions and join in the community of readers. The *Factoring 101 Forums* utilize a standard *Xenforo* bulletin board platform and are very easy to use. The forums are located at:

www.factoringbrokerforums.com

To register for forum use, simply click the "Sign Up Now" button and complete the short sign up form. You will receive an email verification once your registration is complete.

The broker forums are a professional community and we require the use of real names. You may upload an avatar and customize your signature and other information.

In addition to providing a community where new brokers can interact with others by posting threads and comments, the forums also act as a bulletin board where industry lenders will post comments, announce special bonus programs, or launch sales contests for brokers, etc.

Finally, the forums provide a "gateway" to three online portals where brokers can access guide updates, additional training, continuing and advanced education, and marketing support materials.

Although the *Factoring Broker Forum* itself is an open community with access available to everyone with an interest in the industry, entry to the online gateways are private IACFB training or support areas and as such, are protected by "permissions". Permissions are granted on an individual basis and must be manually activated by IACFB administrators.

YOUR ACCESS TO THE LEARNING LAB

As the purchaser of *Factoring 101: A Broker's Guide*, you are entitled to full *Learning Lab* gateway access and permissions. It is very easy to access the Lab which provides a great source of continuing education as you develop your factoring consultancy.

Accessing the Learning Lab

As a purchaser of this guide, you have free access to the *IACFB Learning Lab.* The *Learning Lab* contains:

DIRECTORY OF AMERICAN FACTORS AND LENDERS

- Updates and additions made to the *Factoring 101 Training Guide* between printings.
- Informative articles on factoring and other forms of asset-based finance archived to provide a level of continuing education.
- The *Directory of American Factors and Lenders.* The directory currently includes over 500 specialty lenders and sources of asset-based finance with direct links to their websites. The directory will assist you in constructing your own personal lenders directory.
- *Lender Presentations Archive.* This is an archive of several years of IACFB lender presentations in MP3 format.

Although you have free access to the Lab, you will still need permissions. To get your permissions, simply complete the form at:

www.iacfb.org/LabAccess.html

When you complete the form, use your first and last name as well as your current email address. You will also need a **LAB CODE.** Your **LAB CODE** is:

Factoring 101: Business-in-a-Box at the Campus IACFB Annex

Many new industry brokers will come equipped with the special skills required to create the professional marketing materials needed to launch their business. Others will not. For those in need of some assistance, we have created **Business-in-a-Box** at the Annex.

Business-in-a-Box at the Annex is all about marketing and provides new industry brokers with virtually all the tools they need to be up, running, and marketing in just a matter of days. **Business-in-a-Box** at the Annex includes:

- **WEBSITE:** a templated professionally designed factoring broker website complete with invitation (squeeze) page marketing component
- **OFFERS:** booklets and documents included with your website
- **COLD CALL SCRIPTS:** telephone scripts for every occasion
- **EMAIL:** business email (POP3 / IMAP)
- **BROCHURES:** brochure and flyer templates
- **PRESENTATIONS:** workshop *PowerPoint* presentations
- **HANDOUTS:** workshop handouts in PDF format
- **CASE STUDIES:** downloadable PDF Case Studies
- **MORE:** much more

The Campus IACFB Annex is accessible through the *Factoring Broker Forums Portal.* Permissions to access **Business-in-a-Box** are provided by subscription. To find out more, view current pricing, and sign up for the IACFB's **Business-in-a-Box Program** at the Annex, simply visit:

www.iacfb.org/business_in_a_box.htm

202 Continuing Education at Campus IACFB

COMMERCIAL FINANCE CONSULTANT TRAINING

For those brokers ready to take their business to the next level, IACFB offers the 202 Continuing Online Education for Commercial Finance Consultants at Campus IACFB.

Campus IACFB's Continuing Online Education is an advanced studies area and builds on the basic introductory training provided in the Factoring 101 Series Program. The Campus provides advanced training in the following areas:

- **Factoring and Micro-Factoring**
- **Asset-Based Lending**
- **Small Business Administration Financing**
- **Import-Export Trade Finance**
- **Equipment Leasing**
- **Venture Capital**

Additional information and pre-requisite requirements for the 202 Continuing Education Program can be found at www.iacfb.org

Index

CHAPTER 1 QUIZ PAGE 13

1. C
2. D
3. D
4. D
5. C

CHAPTER 2 QUIZ PAGE 54

1. A
2. D
3. B
4. B
5. D
6. D
7. C
8. A
9. D
10. D
11. D
12. A

CHAPTER 3 QUIZ PAGE 94

1. B
2. B
3. B
4. A
5. D
6. C B
7. C
8. B
9. B
10. A

CHAPTER 4 QUIZ PAGE 110

1. A
2. B
3. C
4. B
5. B
6. C
7. C
8. B
9. D
10. C